Rising Sun Melting Mists

Knowledge of Self dispels ignorance

Dwaraknath Reddy

Rising Sun Melting Mists

Knowledge of Self dispels ignorance

Earlier published as
WHISPERS HEARD WITHIN

Dwaraknath Reddy

A Division of Maoli Media Private Limited

Other Books by Dwaraknath Reddy

- Can God Improve My Balance Sheet?
- Diving Deep into Ramana Maharshi's Teachings
- The Dicey Problem Of New Age Science
- The Physics of Karma
- Gentle Breeze, Rustling Leaves
- Death Was Never Born, Life Never Died
- Divya, The Rainbow Child

Rising Sun Melting Mists

is the new title of the old book

Whispers Heard Within

The title has been changed to give a better assessment of the contents to prospective readers.

The old text has not been altered. Eight new articles have been added. The newly designed cover has now replaced the old covers of the books already held in stock.

Rising Sun Melting Mists

First Edition: October 2013

Published By
ZEN PUBLICATIONS
A Division of Maoli Media Private Limited
60, Juhu Supreme Shopping Centre,
Gulmohar Cross Road No. 9, JVPD Scheme,
Juhu, Mumbai 400 049. India.
Tel: +91 9022208074
eMail: info@zenpublications.com
Website: www.zenpublications.com

Book Design: Red Sky Designs, Mumbai

ISBN 978-93-82788-85-0

Contents

Part II: CONTEMPLATIVE

Dedicated to

My Mother of Infinite Love
Who gave me Life

and

My Mother of natural love
who gave me birth

Preface by M.P. Pandit

How shall we place him? A humanist? An emerging poet? Lover of Nature? Word-artist? Seeker of Truth? These questions naturally arise as we read this collection of the author's writings during the last two decades. Actually he is all of them – and more. Whether the reflections presented here are narrative, lyrical or contemplative – as he classifies them – there is one striking note that runs through all, and that is his passion for love which is another face of Truth. No experience of life – and evidently he has had many – leaves him bitter. Even death reveals to him another side of life.

The themes he handles are varied. The way he expresses himself makes us wonder what is the strength of his appeal. Beauty of style? Power of thought? No, it is the authenticity of his experience, psychological and spiritual, that touches the reader and makes him as humble as the writer himself. Whether he speaks of the Guru 'who leaves no footprints' or of prayer with the language of 'tears in the eyes' rather than of 'words upon the lips' or of the trap of solitude, we are in the presence of an ardent seeker. The thinker in him loves precision of expression: Truth, he says, is beyond method. Astrology is indicative, not determinative.

Epigrams abound. Read a few of them:

"A mind that revolts against what it perceives may bring about a revolution; a mind that revolts against its own lack of perception brings about evolution".

"I have heard Your speech in the silence of my heart; I have felt the caressing touch of Your tender fingers in tears trickling down the cheeks".

All may not be cultured enough, evolved enough, to follow the author in each of his contemplations. But every one is certain to benefit in the culture of his soul by reading this book. Let us turn to the pages forthwith and refresh ourselves in the Stream of Saraswathi, Impeller to happy truths (Rig Veda 1.3), in whom the writer has found his great Refuge.

Pondicherry
June, 25th '85

Bhagavan Shri Ramana Maharshi

Two Words

Swami Chinmayananda

35, College Road
Madras-600 O06
India
17th May 1985

Dwarak is dear to me. He had the guts to give up the chair of his vast and flourishing personally owned company to his nephew whom he had trained, and retire to the quiet life of sadhana at Sri Ramana Maharshi's ashram in Tiruvannamalai.

He had studied Vedanta, reflected upon its wisdom and had meditated long upon its deepest truth. His modern ideas chastened with his "knowledge" is what we have here.

He has a style of his own, pure, chiselled, shaped and carved, to express the intricate beauty of his soaring thoughts. Read these crisp essays, and while enjoying the poetic-prose dive deep, in your own independent reflections, between lines and often between phrases, to reach the "unsaid"

Love

(Sd/-)

Swami Chinmayammda

Swami Chinmayananda

Shri Nisargadatta Maharaj

A NOTE ON THE THIRD EDITION

This collection of articles, many of which were written in the early sixties, was first published under the banner of Bharatiya Vidya Bhavan in 1985 with the title "PAADA POOJA (Worship of Feet Divine)". In this revised and enlarged reprint, some articles written subsequently have also been included. A few amongst them havc appeared earlier in issues of "THE MOUNTAIN PATH", the esteemed magazine of Sri Ramanashramam, Tiruvannamalai. For permission to reproduce them here I express my gratitude to the President of the Ashram, Sri V.S. Ramanan.

PAADA POOJA was intended to signify the offering of love and joy at the feet of the Masters whose teachings and exemplary living had awakened me into a heightened consciousness. But it was later observed that the title was offen wrongly interpreted by prospective readers as being suggestive of ritualism and ordained worship. This was an avoidable misconception of the truth of the contents. Therefore the title of the book has been changed to:

WHISPERS HEARD WITHIN

The sunshine of Grace is ever present in the divine dispensation. Life, for everyone and everywhere, is not without its content of tears. Yet, if one looks with right understanding at the workings of Providence in the totality of creation, one becomes aware of an all-encompassing justice. It can be sensed and felt as a loving living protection of righteousness. And thus even in the hours of sorrow sunshine sparkles through the tears. Reflecting this fact of life, this book also appeared earlier with the title "SUNSHINE IN A TEAR-DROP." At that time, *"whispers heard within"* was the subtitle. Now that has been preferred as the main title.*

**P.S. The new title is 'Rising Sun, Melting Mists'.*

Introduction

He was thirty-seven, I was thirty-five. Our skies were blue, our horizons free of clouds. Yet he, my brother, died. Always together as children, students and young men, now sharing hopes and ambitions and the responsibilities of a promising family business, it seemed that our outstretched hands could pluck the stars.

Then there was the head-ache ("got some aspirin?") soon turning to an agonizing torture, and in the nursing home the dreaded words are whispered: Cerebral haemorrhage. Surendranath is dying.

I am by his side, watching without believing, when an almost imperceptible nod of the drooping head signals the meeting of two eternities of life and of death.

It is over. Just like that....

A betrayal, or a fulfillment? Chaos or harmony? Callousness or kindness? I have to know the rationale of death. Death will return – he always does – for another or for me, and when he does I cannot again let myself be crushed and confused. Before that I must learn the laws that bind both Death and me. Are there laws?

Thus it was that I joined the vast audiences to whom Swami Chinmayananda was discoursing upon mind and matter, work and worship, creature and creator, love and lust, shadow and substance. In essence the teaching was that the limited and conditioned was me; the same me unlimited and unconditioned was all that the word GOD was endowed with in the vocabularies of mankind! The suggestion and the possibility exploded within me and the echoes chanted:

"Good Lord! You are hiding deep inside me closer than I would ever suspect, while I scan the skies for you. I remain the heir to everything even while I long to possess." It became overwhelmingly important that I aspire to the truth of myself.

The expositions of Swamiji laid the foundations of my understanding. And then a protective providence led me to the recorded words of Ramana Maharshi. Only a few words, but each one a ringing chime that lingered within the heart, shutting the sounds outside, and drawing life's energy onto itself – words of promise, words of power, words of proof. What mattered that I had not seen Him in the body, that I had not heard His voice, when His authority possessed me?

If in spite of this brave and not insincere assertion a shadow of regret lay across my mind, physical presence of perfection too was granted to me when a decade later I came across the book "I Am That." Therein Maharshi was speaking again in the form of Nisargadatta Maharaj, a Sage residing in Bombay, this time in personal intimate dialogues, indulgently permitting argument, patiently correcting the perspective, ruthlessly exposing the memorized fallacies. On my visits to Bombay I could sit near Him, indeed as near as my mind would let me.

From 1960 when the startled mind first questioned the powers that be, till 1983, I carried on my duties as Chairman and Managing Director of the family concern, as guardian of my brother's children and as the parent of two daughters and a son. In these years Death was a regular visitor that returned for my father, my younger brother, my mother and my wife. I know that face of Death too well, and with no rancour, for I also know the law Death compulsively obeys. The grace that had reached me through Swami Chinmayananda and Ramana Maharshi, and Nisargadatta Maharaj, kept burning within me the greater purpose of existence, while I gave my mental faculties unreservedly to my business which prospered beyond expectations.

Then in 1983 it seemed that the harmony of events was sanctioning my withdrawal from worldly activity, and in a simple natural effortless transformation I could make my home near Ramanashramam and deal more purposefully, more serenely, with the spiritual content of myself, as my only quest.

Mostly during 1962 – 1964 and to some extent around 1980, I wrote articles on philosophical themes, whose primary purpose was the clarifying and consolidating of my ideas for my progress. Those that were published earlier were for a close and related circle of readers. In the tranquil leisure of my present life, I could collect most of the scattered and forgotten pages to revise and edit them. The warm delight of friends amongst the devotees here, and the appreciation of Swami Chinmayananda, and Sri M.P. Pandit encouraged me to bring out this book.

Along with many that are seekers like myself, I am one student in a large class. At the most, I have striven and done my home-work a little better. I am willing to share my notes happily with you!

DWARAKNATH REDDY

Sri Ramanashramam
Tiruvannamalai – 606 603

Tamil Nadu May 1985

Comments

"WHISPERS HEARD WITHIN" is a collection of emotional and contemplative pieces about which SWAMI CHINMAYANANDA, the widely known and highly regarded exponent of Hindu philosophy in India and the West, wrote to the author:

"Your expressions have a ring and are rich in their deep suggestiveness. I enjoyed the articles... each an Upanishadic canto..."

Sri. M.P. PANDIT, renowned author, philosopher, and the doyen amongst reviewers of spiritual books, wrote from Sri Aurobindo Ashram, Pondicherry, in a personal letter:

"It is more than delightful to go through these prose-poems... forceful in transmitting experience... some of the ideas stay and reverberate... Mr. Reddy, let us share in the bounty you are blessed with, more amply..."

PART I

LYRICAL

I
The Blind One

The mind is created by and contained in concepts of relativity, and the world as it is known is the total of sense perceptions. The ultimate reality is an Absolute, beyond the grasp of senses which can only operate within relativity. Words deal only with mental concepts. Complete and lasting happiness (called Bliss) is found in self-awareness which is independent of sensed knowledge.

If a little girl born blind were to ask you: "What colour is the wind?" how would you answer her?

So asked one lady of me at a party and whether I replied at all I do not now recollect. I presume that in the manner of casual conversations, one subject followed so close upon another's heels that questions were not intended to elicit answers.

When I thought I was alone again, the little blind girl stepped out of dreamy imagination, sat smiling by my side, turned up to me an unseeing face, and gently asked: What colour is the wind?

I said to myself: What is 'colour' to her? She knows not what she talks, but uses words as she has heard others use them. My world is composed of experiences derived from the five senses of touch, taste, sight, smell and sound. She who was born blind has a world composed of four perceptions only. Yet her world must be as complete to her as mine is to me. How mistaken is he who would grieve for one blind from birth, thinking "Alas, must this one remain year after year in darkness?" For, what is darkness to such a one? Awareness of light and existence in darkness, would have been an awesome burden to bear. One who lost sight during one's life, and retained the memory of vision once enjoyed, might suffer from recollections, but one who has never known light is free from the choking bondage of darkness too. You, little girl, have no sorrow, but only confusion over words that were not intended for you. Never mind, we will make those sounds suit your perceptions. Let the words that were developed as symbols for five senses be endowed for you with connotations of your four senses only.

Oh God, help me now. What I am saying is as true as any truth that can be known by the mind. A mind that is the product of four senses is no less perfect than the mind produced by five. Indeed, it may well be closer to Perfection. Give sincerity to my voice that this blind girl may know my answer is completely true and truly complete and that I do not speak in jest.

Then I turned towards her, and without sadness said: I will tell you what colour is the wind. It is the colour of the softness of a rose petal upon your cheek. It is the colour of the coolness of a mountain stream in spring. It is the colour of the song of birds timidly knocking upon the doors of silence as you lie half-awake. It is the colour of the fragrance of summer showers upon the thirsty land. Such is the colour of wind, my child.

And she smiled radiantly, saying: "I know". Yes, she knew it all along, for what else could have been the colour of wind?

Lord, what trickery is this? Is my world complete because I can see, smell, hear, touch, and taste? Can I ever know in what ways I am incomplete? If five senses are possessed, are fifty not possible? My world has no greater claim to perfection for being the total of five senses, than the world revealed to the blind, or the deaf or the mute. The world is not an absolute reality, but is what is known to be. There is cause for neither sorrow nor joy in this. Happiness is independent of knowledge of things, for it abides in Self-Awareness, whereas mental knowledge rests in relativity.

As she rose to leave, she clasped my hand which lay in her lap and said: Thank you.

I watched her go... Did you hear that, good Lord? – She is thanking me! It is I that must thank you child, for you have made me realize only now that I am blind.

2
Let Us Pray

Let us pray. It is the hour of awakening.

Dawn has stirred beyond the distant horizon, and already Night has received an uneasy awareness of the coming light. Hastily she is folding up her dark tent, she dare not tarry longer.

The seeds are sprouting. The measured tread of Time has begun again. Cause, which had lain helpless while deprived of its substratum and sustenance, Time, is moving again into manifestation as effect. Space is every-where! Existence is complete! – for minds have begun to function again, their sleep ended.

Life is on the move. The breeze blows cool and caressing; the branches toss their leafy manes in gay abandon, the birds twitter and flap their wings in sheer ecstasy.

Movement everywhere: Growing and still growing, gathering, expanding, till it is a wave, a surge, a relentless upheaval. Movement within movement. And movement upon movement. And it aught seems to be still, it only seems, for nothing has escaped the deluge. Beware, Time is on the move!

Let us pray to the Force and the Fury. Let us pray to the vastness and the variety. I am a tiny speck gazing in awe and wonder at the might and majesty and terrifying grandeur of Creation. Oh Lord, let me anchor myself to Thy Feet. In Space, I am an atom, and in Time, an instant. Thou alone art the multitude so vast that who shall know all Thy forms? I set forth upon a raft to traverse the ocean across and along, but when I found myself rimmed by the sky all round, with no land in sight, I realized my limitations and the limitlessness of what I had presumed to unravel. Thy grace alone led me across the pathless waters back to the shore I had ventured from in my ignorance. Prayer was my compass and Faith my lodestar. I remember it now, as once again the ocean reveals itself to my gaze and the waves beckon to me with promise of sweet excitement. Wanderlust tugs at the heart-strings and memory deceives, holding forth the joy and thrill of an earlier launching, but hiding the fear, panic, and pained helplessness that followed. Too soon and too easily will I forget how the tears fell from my eyes into the sea, as though the tiny salt-drops could claim kinship with the fathomless brine and plead mercy. The sea rolled on unconcerned, too mighty to pause for a tear or two – but Thou, my Lord, that art incomparably vaster and mightier than all the seas and winds and mountains combined, would not let a tear roll in vain on to Thy Feet.

Then I realized that the Law is helpless too for all its size and stature. Turn to the Lawgiver.

Let us pray, remembering this at dawn, watching the wave of Life gathering, growing, sweeping outward.

Let us pray. It is the hour of dusk. Look upon the benign face of Sandhya[1] as she moves gently, holding day with one hand and night with the other.

---

1 The hour when day yields to night

The wave is returning, no longer a mighty flood, but a diminishing calmness. Gone is the mad rush outward, this is home-coming, a getting back to the source. One by one the noises are stilled. The wind lies hushed, the birds have sung their songs, the children leave their play-grounds to nestle in the laps of their mothers.

Oh Lord, how weary, stale and lonesome is this existence without Thee. I am tired, tired beyond endurance.

All is here. Out there, there is nothing. The going out was folly.

Thus let us pray at dusk, seeing the involution, the folding back of the macrocosm into the microcosm. And when the merger is completed, the revelation will await us that the microcosm is itself the macrocosm, and the law-giver am I, I was never lost on a tiny raft in a mighty ocean, it was all a dream or perhaps less than a dream.

Oh God, let thoughts subside with the fading light. Let quiet reign within the once-turbulent chest. Peace be. Om Shanthi... Shanthi... Shanthi.

3
At a Wedding

The earnest seeker who wonders whence and how creation arose must be guided into the higher understanding using his own terms and values. We see beings as creations from the union of the male and the female. The seed is from the Father, the evolution and emergence is from the Mother.

So the ancient wisdom has shown the One in many aspects, and given us the varied imagery of gods and goddesses and divinities. The one omnipotent God is seen as Shiva (the Potential), Sakthi (the energy that can manifest), and the world (the manifested). Yet He is the celibate too (Brahmachari) forever Alone!

Shiva weds Sakthi and Thought is created! Then there is, and need be, nothing else besides, for the universe, nay, even time and space, are not other than the contents of thought, and thus the process of continuous manifestation is set in motion, as the thought flow of cosmic consciousness.

> *The Reality of every being is itself the total truth of God. Therefore every wedding has in itself all the grandeur and power of the faculty and urge that created the universe – that created creation.*
>
> *When all this is recognized, humanity can retain its goal and aspiration – but we have merely preserved the ritual and lost the* meaning at our weddings in this age.

Unasked, memory sets up a refrain: "Oh Lord, forgive them, for they know not what they do."Over and over, the line runs through the mind, while watching fantasies and friends streaming into the decorated marriage-hall.

They stream into the *pandal* (enclosure), multitudes of them, smiling men and bedecked women, awkward youths and self-conscious girls, and playful children.

To see. To be seen. To see being seen. To be seen seeing. Yes, but what besides? Where is the substance?

To hark back to the beginning of Time? To become aware of awareness? To bless?

He and she. Each incomplete and seeking fulfillment. Caught in the fantasy that this is the way, the return to unity, the recapture of bliss. Alas, the fallacy.....the mistake that addition can eliminate.... the attempt to gain mastery over vastness by understanding all the pluralistic components, while the riddle lies solved in the total comprehension of any one of the units. To try to see the end of numbers by reaching for the ultimate numeral, while,all the time, the zero wraps up the secret within its circle and laughs at the foolish mind.

He and she. Choosing to unite. Nay, not even free to choose, but compelled to this end by the creative urge that started when time started, or rather, before it; for, was not Time created? And deluded into thinking that matter exists and is the truest medium for the expression of the creative faculty. Look at them limiting themselves, limiting each other, self-willed exiles from kingdoms of the Self.

Look at them again, and blame them not. You, Lord, are to blame. We have wept at many a funeral and sung at many a wedding, whereas not without reason we might have feasted at funerals and wailed at the weddings. But you started the clinging misconception that The Only One needed another, and the other could be found beyond! And you will not end this fooling.

So the moment arrives. Once there was a wedding at which the music was the surging of the four winds through space, to the thundering accompaniment of clashing worlds. Now the breath flows through the flute and little fingers dance upon the drum. We are back at the instant when the Eternal Brahmachari pretended that femininity was a fact, and the Mother played at being a maid!

There is joy in every heart. In some there is wistful sadness of remembrance, which is as pure a joy as any they have known. In others, there is a welcome pain of anticipation more soothing than any glee of earlier days. So, some are incomplete through having lost, and some through not yet having gained, but happily they are all incomplete and thereby capable of yearning for experience of joy!

Is sorrow different?

The fire burns, the fire of life, sustained by sacrifice, nurtured by yagna-spirit. The union shall be blessed... thrice blessed for body, mind and intellect; thrice blessed for the three states of consciousness;[2] thus three times blessed. And finally, grains of rice dyed in saffron placed upon the head, with a prayer: "May they transcend into the Fourth plane of Turiya"... at least the rituals remain...

Shiva and Sakthi... Purusha and Prakriti... He and She...

On to the deceptive smoothness of the sea of samsar[3] glides yet another boat, with sails gently caressed by warm zephyrs.

2 Waking, dream, and deep-sleep are the three states of our experience. TLIRIYA is the supreme state of Absolute Awareness, transcending the other three.

3 Worldly existence.

4
The Secret

Krishna, I ask you:

Why am I made to suffer over and over the deception of sugar in the palm that turns to sand in the mouth? Of promises to the mind that are broken to the heart?

You smile that enigmatic smile that is like sunshine while it is still raining.

And well you might, for long ago you answered these same questions, and I should know the answers too well:

I suffer because I choose to remain incomplete. I am hurt because I refuse to abandon pain.

I am deceived because I demand.

I am lost in the banality of words and talk lightly of surrender, while I cling to the conviction that only my own strength can be my succour.

I chant "Thy will be done", but believe action originates from my will!

Where is trust in all this?

As long as I seek,
I cannot find

As long as I stare,
I will be blind.

5
The Farewell

Each in her and his mind is thinking: The moment we knew was arriving too fast, yet hoped would never arrive, is now upon us. The days of being together have run their course, and too suddenly the sweet indulgence has turned to sadness. In vain, it seems now, is the attempt to cling to the words that gave us courage and comfort, the mocking echoes have no substance and our fingers clutch at emptiness. You are there still, and these eyes can behold the form, so all is not lost yet, but which way shall we turn for solace when you have moved beyond the horizon? Where shall we search for light when engulfed in darkness? It were kinder to have no eyes and know not darkness, than to have eyes and know not light.

Tick, tock, tick, tock... Relentlessly the hands move across the dial. We are gathered in this railway station bound by a common love, and thereby destined to share a common grief. The train is standing there, ominously motionless, but it seems to be alive and restive, like a horse yielding to the rein but resenting the curb on its freedom.

You stand at the door of the carriage... Smiling.

Smiling and smiling and smiling...

Is love one thing and sadness another? Who has loved, knows the answer; knows it in tears dearly bought, knows it in scars secretly worn. How shall we fetch forth our answering smiles, if only to pay you our tribute in a desperate show of courage? Alas, our smiles lie buried beneath the debris of castles that suddenly collapsed in our hearts.

The wheels will turn now. Grinding merciless wheels. Waging their bitter battle against hard rails that will not yield. Steel on steel. Nothing asked, nothing given. What matter to them that hearts are caught in between? When steel challenges steel and steel resists steel, is there even the slightest cognizance of a tenderness caught betwixt?

If time would stop! If time could be stopped! If this moment could be forever...

It was then that your smile spoke to us, and these the words I heard in the silence of your gaze:

Time can be stopped. But not by these tears. When love is changed to tears, what remains? There is only emptiness, not the power of love.

One rail is the past, the other the future. Riding astride is the train, the Present. Memory as recollection informs, and memory as desire activates, the Present movement. Time in movement is the mind. A stilled mind is free from time.

This stillness can be sleep which gains nothing. Or, it can be love which leaves nothing ungained. Not a love circumscribed, which must then encounter the excluded upon a frontier, and be destroyed by fear of the unknown. But a fearless love that is a centre without a circumference and therefore not a centre at all. Not a love between, just love. Not moving, just pervading. Not love in you, just you.

Bring about this transformation in yourself. Gone then are the rails of past and future and the truth of Time is seen to be not an eternity of change but a changeless Eternity.

Love has the power to unearth the rails, and without rails where shall the train go? Love can never lose. The heart of the Lover holds the Beloved captive.

6
Home At Last

At journey's end I am groping through the dense darkness of a wintry new-moon night to reach an unseen destination. The shuffling feet feel their way past the thorns and the stubbles and the jutting stones. Not without hurt and pain, but with determination I WILL my progress, having nowhere to stop and no time to lose.

Suddenly a streak of lightning cleaves the night from cloud to clod, a forked fury hissing at the darkness, too too brief its duration, too too bright its intensity. Was its intent to be kind? Or was it only to strike me blind?

Till then, blinded by darkness I was moving somehow, but when blinded by light I stumbled and fell. Had I been only robbed of my strength, strength would have returned; but robbed of hope, I lay still.

Home is where the journey ends. And the end is where, having given up personal hatred, you learn to give up personal love. Upon the journey you know that darkness can blind you. The journey ends when you know that light can blind you more.

And THAT is sight... that is SIGHT.

7
Not Lonely – Just Alone

What have I known of what can be known of Brahman, if not that there is nothing besides? That It alone is all that is, was, or can be?

So how can I be surprised that the growth and the movement of the seeker is into an Aloneness, serene, silent, joyous?

Why then this hurt? Is it that I assumed I could choose and decide the sequence and timing of my disenchantments, but found myself being robbed today of what I would willingly part with tomorrow – like a tree that intends to shed the autumnal leaves one by one, but finds itself stripped and stark naked from one sudden gust?

So be it then, oh Lord, that I may become aware of Thy Hand in the crucial turn of my life. But I will not pretend that it does not hurt. How strange and sad, my Lord, that my follies were extolled and my failures were applauded, but when the ultimate offering of my chastened soul was placed before the people that I loved, they spurned it and crushed it under a heel!

Lord, did I think that I could go to them with my tears and then come to you with my smiles? Forgive my foolishness, for now I know!

I have nothing to give but tears, and I have no one to give them to but Thee.

8
The Recovery

Obviously it is the human that needs to be divinised, it is the unclean that must be cleansed, the suppliant that must be supported. To whom is pardon if not to the penitent?

Will you refuse me the helping hand when I reach out on tip-toe? Will you distrust me now when I lay bare my soul? Will you punish me when I stand with folded hands?

Will you hold against me what I have abandoned when I plead for acceptance? Will you shut the doors of the sanctum sanctorum in my face even as, on weary feet, I struggle into the precincts of your temple?

Here is the garland of random hues that I strung together with the wild flowers I gathered in my wanderings. It is the miscellany of my life. If I cannot leave it with you, what shall I do with it?

I believed the world owed me happiness, but when I raved and demanded, derisive silence was the answer. Oh God, what price will memory extract from those who will be her slaves, holding out the promise of delights to their trusting minds and breaking it to their hearts!

Phantom mists of remembered things, be gone. Beyond you is a void that will bend my sight back upon its source, where enshrined stands the Divine, patiently anticipating recognition and smiling mysteriously.

9
Living in Sadhana

Sadhana is normally understood to be the systematized practice of ritual or study or meditation by the earnest seeker of spiritual salvation. The wavering and often revolting mind has to be disciplined through chanting of mantras, telling of beads, floral offering, worship at shrines, singing of hymns, meditation. All these help, they are beautiful, purposeful, necessary. But the awakened mind that has sensed the essential nature of Reality and glimpsed the laws of existence and action, goes beyond scheduled procedure and ordained performance into a constant remembrance of the changeless Substratum behind the changing phenomena.

Through such a mind the seeker sees his timeless continuity in his daily resurgence at dawn, his serene tranquility despite a tempest of desires, his actionless poise amidst endless movement, and his subjective supremacy when objectivity sleeps. His whole life is itself Sadhana.

Another day dawns. Time swiftly rolls away the dark carpet of Night and unfolds a new vista of colour and cadence, of delight and despair, of hope and horror. My soothing slumber is ended. I am awake, alert, agitated. My life is measured by dawn and dusk, and each day hauls me a step nearer to my grave. I am carried as driftwood in a torrent. So it seems.

And then I think: No womb ever held Me, so no tomb can ever hold Me either. It is Time, not I, that was born, It is Time that marches towards Death. The movement is not in me, but around me. Staying still, I see no ripples upon the placid expanse of Time. I have loaned to it my stillness, by becoming still myself.

Thus I think – that is Sadhana.

With sprightly step, I stride across the meadow. And suddenly – look! See how gracefully she stands, a maiden of ageless beauty, the fairest blossom upon the land, youth in every limb, litheness in every movement, laughing as the breeze caresses her flowing tresses. She stands there, supremely confident of the spell she casts, mocking manhood with a flicker of an eyelid.

And then I say: Mother, bewitching is your play of forms. But I am formless. Bereft of memory, I am neither male nor female, neither young nor old, nor fair nor dark. Am I this body, that other bodies can be meaningful to its desperate demands? I am that point of Awareness that discerns in one careless sweep the panorama of the sunlit grassy slopes upon which stands the sullen and alluring girl, staring at this other body. Mother, keep me indifferent.

Thus I say – that is Sadhana.

I launch myself into activity. There are things I must do, duties that beckon to me, and there is eager anticipation of the fruits of action, held in the clenched fist of Time called the future. The hope of success is at once also the fear of failure. I am deceived by the frailty of friendships, I am distracted by unexpected encounters, I am dismayed by my own inadequacies. How shall I bear the burden of unrequited desires, if my labours yield not the fruits that prompted them?

And then I remember: What is action to me? There is nothing I need to do. Action fulfils itself in an ancient and everlasting cascade of causation, a victim of its own laws, and foolishly swallows the fruit to perpetuate the seed. But I am merely a witness to this pulsating play of light and shadow or its total cessation. What shall the ocean gain through the flooded river or lose through the vapourous cloud? Let such action flow through me as is decreed by the harmony of my presence in my environment, but I am not the one who acts. Deeds may be done, but I do nothing.

Thus I work - that is Sadhana.

Another day departs, adding a leaf to memory. The pleasures obtained must be recalled, the pains endured must be banished. But I lack the sovereignty either to recall the one, or to banish the other. I am tired, so tired. I no longer want to think, yet I cannot stay awake and stop thinking. Sleep is my only solace, into sleep I must dissolve.

And then I see: I do not dissolve into sleep. I preside over sleep. The mind will end, the thoughts will end, while Time will lie still in suspended animation. But I, who was tossed and tormented by their conspiracy will stand as sole survivor. Shall I not stay thus for ever more? The puny ego "I" that locks itself within the mind cannot even seek the soothing comfort of sleep, except that a kindly Grace leads it beyond the labyrinth of willing and wishing, and lays upon its bruises the happy unction of forgetfulness. But I, dear God, that am the Truth of Thee and Me, what is sleep to me that wakefulness was not?

Thus I see – I see and smile and close my eyes – that is Sadhana.

10
On Faith

Some say that Faith is the essence of spirituality, or even all of it. Others say that faith is an insult to the intellect. Both are right: For, it is not of one concept that they are talking. One is talking of the farthest frontiers of the Intellect, the other of conclusions which have not been subjected to analysis and discrimination. Thus, it often happens that we use one and the same word, yet mean entirely different things by it, and so enter into arguments that cannot obviously be resolved.

What has come to pass is available as Knowledge. It is only that which is yet unmanifest that can be an object of faith. Therefore, agreed that faith can be called blind. To say so is not to decry faith, but to define it. By definition, it must be unseen to be faith; to say that faith is blind is to say what is grossly redundant. What is more to the point is to decide how far an attitude of faith is in accordance with an intelligent view of life.

It has become fashionable for the educated to say of themselves that they cannot accept anything on faith. The implication is that talk of God is vague by their standards of material assertions, and that His existence cannot be proved by their senses. Therefore, they conclude that those who will surrender everything to attain liberation, are only kneeling at the altar of an unproved faith, which gains sustenance from the credulity of their own deluded minds.

Yet these very people are constantly existing in faith, and because of faith. When they breathe air, they are demonstrating their faith in the quality of air to flow into the lungs and to sustain life. When they eat food, do they not testify to their faith that the material they take into their bodies will, by complex metabolism, convert itself to become part of their blood, bones and sinews ? When they wave a merry farewell with a pledge to meet on the morrow, do they not imply their faith in the coming of the morrow and the dawn of another day ? Whence, then, their disdain of faith as a component in the basic mechanics of life itself ?

They will answer: "But it has always been thus. Air has at all times sustained life, and food has nurtured the body. The sun has ever risen at the appointed hour. This is but the rationale of the known".

But they are assuming that the rationale will hold in future, are they not? They accept without question that the laws governing the universe are enduring and changeless, do they not ?

This is the essence of Faith, to know that natural laws will not change while Time remains as what it is. Faith is not a content of the mind: in truth, mind is the content held in Faith. Things known constitute the mind. What gives validity in "future" to that which came to be known in the "past" is Faith. Were it not for Faith, there could be no knowledge. Divine Justice would be perpetually suspect, the Karmic law would be called into question, and Time would no longer be what we know it to be, for, when there is no continuity, where is Time ?

Faith is the recognition of Dharma, the cardinal aspect of which is that all things will, at all times, be true to their nature. To know this is to know how serene and unruffled is Nature, to know that unvaried speed is the only stillness known to relativity, that Shanti is the centre of the revolving wheel. To have faith in these conclusions is but to engender a vaster faith that there must be Stillness unrelated to motion, and a Shanti that is not circumscribed by a circle. To have witnessed the formation of a lake is to have acquired faith in the concept of the sea.

It is when one expects results that are out of harmony with nature, that we have an instance of what might justifiably be termed "blind faith". If a beggar, who puts forth no constructive labours, entertains a faith that one day he will be a millionaire, he but harbours a blind faith. If one believed that a certain offering at a particular shrine will automatically cure a malady, that too is blind faith, for, if the cure is to be the effect, the cause (says the law) must be the thoughts at the time of worship, and not the mere ritual of actions. At the same time, it must be understood, that the faith, wrongly reasoned though it be, may be so strong as to generate the right thoughts of total surrender, with the result that grace is thereby attained, or still more correctly, what is attained is identified as Grace and the gift of God.

On the other hand, the certainty that pure and selfless love can accomplish whatever it seeks, that single-pointed thought achieves its objective, is faith that will for ever fulfill itself, for it is entirely in tune with the laws that function through mind and matter.

Faith, experienced by man, without which he cannot live, is a flicker and fragment of the boundless Faith in Himself with which Brahman, the One, manifested fearlessly as many to create cosmic plurality. And from the heart of man the tiny spark reaches out in kinship to the mighty conflagration from which it arose. Faith will render the re-merger a fact.

So with Faith let us march forward. It is the guiding light. And who ever heard of light being blind?

II
Paada Pooja

The individual, as yet imperfect, is the statue, a frozen frame in time. I am the ego of the individual, with the potential for Perfection. The girl is the soul of Nature, simple, loving, uninhibited, joyous. Her own perfection moulds the mind of the responding individual. The aspiring ego would offer obeisance to the harmonious beauty of nature's law, while Nature herself acknowledges the Perfection that begot her, and which she beholds.

Her faith bursts into an awakening that restores the right identities and blows Time away. Light of true knowledge dispels the darkness of ignorance. The Creator (Purusha) is worshipped by the created (Prakrithi or Nature)

I am no longer a limited ego. I am He, the Creator. Her faith in me has revealed to me the Fact of Myself.

Yet without the created, there could be no creator.
She who is my devotee, is my architect too!

It was a statue. Being a statue, it was, and had to be, helpless. It preserved a moment for an eternity. One frozen mood was its mind forever. Or else, it could have been a man, waiting.

I was standing aside, close enough, but in the silent shadows. I was seeing, myself unseen.

She came with a dancer's lilting gait. As a diamond has a thousand faces to show, all of them dazzling arrays of light and hue, yet each a fresh wonder of beauty, so did the joy upon her countenance shine and shimmer and shift, but never cease.

She gazed a long while upon that face of the statue. "Oh eyes, you are looking too hard, so you are seeing too much. And that is hurting you. Look lightly, that you may discern the outlines of passing occurrences through the mist of time, whose contours flow and merge and are lost in an endless flux." So saying, she ran her fingers in gentle strokes upon the eyes, which lost their stern fixity, and learnt to see all while seeing nothing. She stepped back from the statue, the better to view, and appraised further what she beheld.

"Oh mouth, why so harsh at the corners? You disapprove, for you demand too much. Have you watched the waves upon the ocean, caused by and causing their own ceaseless continuity of motion, helpless slaves of their mirth and monotony? What demands can they heed? Smile softly at the mind that rises and falls, blown by the breezes of memory, hugging desire to its heaving breast."

Speaking thus, she reached out and pressed her palms upon the lips, which shaped themselves into a suggestion of a smile, with no trace of complaint or expectation, an unmoving witness of an unending movement.

Then she surveyed the figure again and saw that the limbs were tense. "Arms, relax. What deeds must be done, what wars must be won, that you thus bear the burden of awaited work? The planets are moving unaided in their orbits and the howling wind seeks in vain for a haven of rest. The Will stands still while the willed gyrates."

With her hands she gently stroked the rigid arms till the tautness disappeared, and there was an easy grace of strength and power held in rein, born of trust in one's own lordliness.

Then would I have moved from the shadows that had hidden me, to touch the feet of this girl who had put light in the eyes, and a smile on the lips and supple strength in the sinews of a helpless statue. But at that very moment she drew back a little – she who had re-modelled, revived and resurrected the sculptured stone – and in an unmeditated reversal of roles, gave to it her mastery and borrowed from it its limitation, by going down upon her knees and laying her forehead upon its feet.

In that instant the shadows were gone, and the idol crumbled to dust and was quickly blown away. I was standing where the idol had stood, bathed in a blaze of light. I felt a moist touch of kindness in my eyes such as I had never known before. I sensed contentment in my mind that could endure an eternity. I was aware of a quiet strength in all my limbs that could hold Time upon a leash.

And resting her forehead upon my feet was she, my devotee, my architect.

12
The Search

Intent upon searching for Lord Krishna, I raised my voice in adoration of Him and sang with a full throat. The sound rolled forth to East and West, to North and South. It spread along the earth like a carpet and it filled the spaces of heaven. It went farther and farther and was lost in the silence of the far beyond.

Then I waited for Him, waited to hear His Flute call me in tender response, waited to see His fair shape come towards me with gentle step, but He did not call and He did not come.

Sadly trying to understand wherein I had failed, I collected the dispersed melody that I had sent forth, to trace it to its origin and reassess its worth. So from East and West and North and South, from the earth upon which it had unrolled itself, and from the space it had permeated, by an effort of my will, the melody returned to form once again the word upon my lips. And the word retraced its passage through my throat into the deepest recesses of my body. And there I saw for the first time that the word had arisen from an intention, the core of which was silence.

In this silence, I saw Lord Krishna.

I saw His sweet Form, and I heard the Melody of His Flute.

I felt a fulfillment, I felt an emptiness. I seemed to know everything, I seemed to know nothing. I was overcome by love, I was filled with resentment. I had no doubts left, I was too perplexed even to enquire.

At long last I said: "Oh Lord, how do you do this?"

The Lord smiled and said "Through Maya"[4]

After a while, I said" Oh Lord, why, why, why do you do this?" And He burst into peels of laughter; and He spoke through His rocking mirth, so I cannot say I heard Him truly - but I think He said: "For My Leela[5]".

---

4 Maya is the creative power in Omnipotence that can give amazing reality to an illusion.

5 Leela is a joyous abandon in sportive play. See also the note on "The Eternal Link."

13
Love and Forgiveness

Now that he is no more, how will you love him? "We will remember him constantly and forever," they said.

But, remembrance cannot be constant. Only what was forgotten can later be remembered. And what is forgotten frequently even now, how can it remain for ever?

"We love him so dearly, how can we forget him?" they protested.

That is the mistake, to think that what is loved is remembered, and what is remembered is loved. True love must be the highest expression of the mind and Time should not dim its lustre. Constancy can never be expressed through the inconstant mind.

"We have lost his presence. Must we lose the memory too?" they said in their defence.

Do I have to remember who I am? I am ever myself, and so I never cease to be. In myself I am not surprised by time, for I move concurrently with it. It is in my objective experience that I am victimised by time. The fault is not of time, but of perception. Time is one part of my mind. Experience in time and space is the other part. When they move together, there is calm, there is the stillness of relative motion, as of two vehicles moving alongside at the same speed. But we attempt the impossible and come to grief. We try to stop time with memory. We try to arrest the planets in their orbits to capture one moment deemed more precious than all the rest, but the might of the cosmic mind grinds relentlessly and sweeps the favoured moment forward. What avails the anguish of one atom in the vastness of the universe? Know that the universe is itself powerlessly propelled; how then shall it be the dispenser of mercy?

Will you stop time by remembering? You will but court grief. Worse still you will offend that which you seek to revere. You say he was of noble heart, gentle and loving, of cheerful countenance, smiling, and generous of disposition, helping and serving. BECOME HIM. Love is identification, oneness, removal of duality. Let his nobility, cheer and generosity reside in your heart. Thereby memory is not lost, but is transcended. He is no more, but that love of which he was a grand expression has not ceased to be. Merge yourself and that love into an indivisible entity. If his love was the cause, and your happiness the effect, that happiness will turn to a memory, to vain and volatile tears, and will soon vanish. But when love is the cause and love is the effect, that love will be forever.

How will you atone for the wrongs you have done?

"We will repent and ask for forgiveness." they said.

You will have to forgive yourselves. You say you will repent. Does not willful repentance require remembrance of the wrongs? Can constant remembrance of the wrong lead to right?

"What could we do then?" they asked, seeing and not seeing, both at one time.

To have forgotten through transcendence is to stand forgiven. But forgetfulness cannot be willed. It will come of its own accord as we march forward in knowledge. What do we mean when we say "we acted wrongly"? At each moment we act according to the sum-total of our knowledge at that moment. Later, that level of ignorance is eliminated in the ascendance to a higher knowledge which now reveals the inadequacy of a vanquished hour. But in that earlier hour of lower evolution we could not have acted otherwise.

To know this is to be ever forgiven. Or rather, the past is eternally forgiven by the present. KNOWLEDGE FORGIVES IGNORANCE. TRUTH FORGIVES FALSEHOOD. There is no other forgiveness, there cannot be.

"To love, then, we remember forever, without interruption, as it were", they mused, "and to forgive we remember never, without exception. One is memory transcended, the other is memory eliminated. The two would seem to be the farthest removed from each other. Yet, where there is love there is forgiveness, and that which is fully forgiven must be fully loved too. If so, love and forgiveness join hands. How can they, if they are the farthest extremities?" They were questioning themselves.

May be they are the extremities of a circle? If so, would they not join hands?

"It must be so", they cried in sudden delight. "It cannot be any other way."

So saying they left, silent and thoughtful. Mind had come a full circle.

14
A Crucifixion

The methodology of life has this thrust: Desire, action, fulfillment or failure, reaction, and mutation of desire. The cycle never ends, the action never ceases; till some day the ego sees the futility of the quest for abiding happiness through desires satiated or desires subdued, and seeks its true freedom in the total denial of desire.

Mind which can only exist as memory and express as desire, faces annihilation in the resolve of the ego to be desireless. The habituated mind perseveres with individuality in a desperate bid at self-preservation.

But the ego that has glimpsed the dawn of enlightenment knows that death of the mind is the pre-condition for the revelation of immortality. Limited within time and space the ego remains a movement in causation, whereas freed from the chain of continuity the ego is the Eternal, beyond time, beyond space, beyond the conceptualizing mind.

My one leg is Space. The other is Time. These two support my body, which is Causation.

My day is done. My race is run. How fantastic it has all been! I do not remember exactly how it began, but from my earliest recollections till now, I am aware of an endless persecution. Then, as now, I was beleagured by hordes of these diminutive demons. As wild dogs surround and torment a lordly beast of larger stature till, beaten and bruised, he yields to their persistence and is consumed, so these demons have ever attacked me in their thousands, shrieking their shrill notes of hatred and anger.

The demons are desires. I am the ego.

I asserted my strength over the pygmies. I crushed them one by one, I toyed with them and tossed them aloft, I allowed them to hack at me while I smiled complacently like a Gulliver, supremely confident of my towering stature beside the tiny creatures. But I had to learn slowly that their progeny was legion, that they multiplied faster than I could kill or consume them, that their forces grew while mine diminished. I could never destroy them all, never, never.

It was then that suddenly I asked myself why I wanted to fight them. Slowly the answer came to me: "So that I may perpetuate myself." But why should I perpetuate myself in the midst of forces bent upon my destruction? I could find no satisfactory answer.

So I stopped the struggle. I laughed aloud and said ' I have no anger, and no hatred. I will not resist any 1onger." A myriad voices retorted in gay unison: "We will destroy you, destroy you." "Do what you will" I said, "my day is done, my race is run." I remained still.

They came at me, surging throngs of them, seething masses of them. They thrust their little spears into me, they slashed with their little blades at me, they pushed me backwards and backwards to the distant horizon. And there I found rising through the mist, a cross as tall as I.

Who put that cross there? Now I believe there is a cross for each one of us, awaiting us in the mist upon the horizon, for each one of us too is a Christ, small or not so small. To many, it is a symbol of fear, of tyranny, of defeat. But to some it becomes a symbol of a transcendental logic, of conquest, of liberation.

So they set me against the cross, and when I looked around me, I saw that many had disappeared, perhaps finding the sport now mirthless. But those that remained are still here and I see that these are the old faces that have longest troubled me. I know their wrinkled features and their gnarled hands, and the venom of their eyes. They will not rest till they have destroyed me or perished in the effort.

They are driving their nails into my flesh. My legs are red with blood, and my body weary and battered. One by one the demons are falling, consumed by their own exertions, but I know that the last one will not fall till the job is done.

Poor devils, they see in me a threat to their survival. I was no wiser as long as I saw in them a threat to mine. Now, I see them and myself for what we are, and thus seen, there is no anger, no hatred, no desperate clinging to a peaceless existence. Instead, there is a joy that the blood is ebbing out. I sense already a freedom that is not the numbness of sleep, but the superior conscience of an awakened stillness.

Come closer, my friends, and quicker do thy task. I can hardly wait for the fulfillment of thy offering. You think you bring me the gift of Death. How would you know that my surrender has changed it to Immortality!

15
The Knot That Remains

Name and fame, wealth, praise, flattery,
These are the chains that bind me,
Worn as jewels but borne as penance,
Deftly wrought links of gold and silver
And burnished steel that hides its harshness –
All of them the proffered gifts of time,
But I must abandon them now
Before Time lays claim to my mortgaged life,
For too soon it will be too late.
Is it for love of me that Time lavished
This extravagance upon me? Or only
To enslave me through my trust and dependence?

The deceit of Time will be the grin
Of hideous death when it pounces
Upon my trusting mind and robs me
Of all my hoarded possessions in a trice.
But if, alerted now to the treachery,
I can undo the knots of lingering desire
And break the shackles of temptations;

If I can redeem from the usurer
My kingly crown I pawned for tinsel gifts;
If I can surprise Time and await death
Serenely secure in my own innate bliss;
What can I not lay aside without pain?
What shall I want to hold for added gain?

You, only you.

Let all the stars be swept from the skies,
Let all the flowers wither upon their boughs,
Let the joys of a life-time turn barren
And memories drop away like autumn leaves,
Yet you will remain, your lovely face
Too deeply etched for all the veils
Of forgetfulness to dim or hide.
What can I do?
If this be the tribute that Time will extract
From one who would rise in revolt,
If this be the cross I can never lay down
Till I sleep smiling upon its thorns,
So let it be, and let it be proclaimed
That time did win. But I did not lose.

16
My Gurudev

Must I say in words what I would sooner cherish in the secret sacred stillness of my heart – what Gurudev means to me? And if I must, how shall I do it? How does anyone ever express the transcendental? What can I express with words that are all fury and no achievement, words that are mere pygmies from the petty kingdom of Sound, gnawing ineffectually at the towering mountain of Silence? I think there are words in some deep recess within me that are yet unknown to language, even unknown to sound... I feel their embryonic flutter as I struggle for expression.

I sit upon the bank and watch the river flow by, carrying in its flood endless variety of shapes and forms. Some struggle and cry in fear "Let me live, let me live" but they go under, a faint ripple marking momentarily the end of their pilgrimage on earth. Before long, even that passes away, and the smooth waters glide unconcerned with deceptive serenity. Some go laughing by, happy and playful, till they and their laughter recede beyond the horizon, and the sudden silence leaves one in ominous doubt whether they and their laughter have already ceased, or have yet a little way to go. Some float by too lost in stupor to know their fate, much less to care, and they sink here or yonder, it matters not. Once in a rare while, mercifully not oftener, there passes the gnarled countenance of one who grabs a weak victim and suffocates him as though he decides who alone will survive, but a moment later that one too vainly seeks desperate protection as the derisive waters part and unite, and a glossy innocence hides another secret.

I watch this dismal awesome unending procession, and suddenly wonder why I am not a part of it. I realize then that my body is wet and the water is dripping from my hair. I must have been drifting all too recently in the river myself. How was I saved?

I turn around and look up and there I look into the face of Benevolence. Therein is a tenderness like the soft light of a candle. Therein is a radiance like that of the eastern sky at dawn. Therein is a fragrance like that of a dew-kissed rose.

I cling to His feet, and He smiles. He smiles for the dead and the living. He smiles for the river and the bank. Nothing is said. Nothing remains unsaid.

Gurudev, I know not what you are. I know but a thousandth part of Thy Grace. Tears in the eyes must speak for me, not words upon the lips.

17
The Lord's Grace

Not that there have never been moments of grace, there have. Moments when diffused lightning dimly flashed and held back for an instant the oppressive darkness.

Or else, dear Lord, how could one bear the burden of knowledge lacking altogether the fulfillment of experience? Faith itself would falter on its forward journey, if looking timidly over the shoulder, it could not discern its footprints!

So in Thy Mercy and Thy Love, Thou has not withheld glimpses. Once, a drum-beat entered my heart and grew and grew till I could contain it no longer, and when it emerged, it was You, dancing, whirling, vibrating – in fun, in joy, in fury, in ecstasy – till the motion rose into a frenzied crescendo that seemed motionless – so still, so silent, so imperceptibly vibrant. Then, when I and my heart were reunited, Thy grace had left me a little wiser and a lot in love.

Have I not seen You dimly outlined before my closed eyes, flute in hand, gently smiling? Have not sudden tears sprung forth unasked to wash with gratitude Thy tender Feet?

But recognition halts the manifestation, and desire for more puts an end to it. What shall I do? Thy Grace, not my will, can reveal Thee to me. But my mind rushes forth, only to see Thy Grace recede. I defeat myself and drive away the love that would be mine.

Then let me understand this. Every new thought is knowing the hitherto unknown. How can I know the unknown? It is like waking up. How can I wake up from deep sleep? Surely not by my effort, for there can be no effort in the deep sleep condition. My will cannot enter there. Obviously, change from one plane of consciousness to another cannot be the result of will. The pot cannot hold water outside itself. The will, limited and conditioned by the extent of knowledge now available to the mind, cannot lead the mind beyond those frontiers. Since every thought subsides into nescience while the next thought arises as a new plane of consciousness, an awakening from the sleep of ignorance into the dawn of new cognition, movement of thought can only be an act of Grace.

All then is Thy Grace. There is nothing besides. Through a timeless play, wherein You made me seemingly aware of fleeting moments of contact with You and phantom glimpses, You have now made me understand that You were ever residing in my own heart.

It only remains that I believe without faltering. The search is ending, Krishna, the long and weary search... I feel descending upon me a peace I never knew before.

18
THE CRY OF THE SEEKER

OM ASATO MA SAT GAMAYA!
TAMASO MA JYOTIR GAMAYA!
MRTYOR MA AMRTAM GAMAYA!

Om, Lead me from unreality to Reality!
Lead me from darkness to Light!
Lead me from death to Immortality!

Such was the prayer of the anguished soul, chastened by the repeating inadequacy of its quest for abiding peace, and at last able to discern that a wrong methodology cannot lead to the right solution. For so long had I sought enduring happiness in relationships and possessions, and blindly believed that passing time would ultimately bestow upon me the gift of bliss. Grown wiser I now pray for redemption, humbly conceding the fallacy of my age-old convictions.

I describe my present state as ASAT, untrue, a negation of reality. And I beseech to be lead to SAT, truth, positivity.

But falsehood and truth, unreality and reality, have both been aspects of my knowledge and experience all my life. They are words I am familiar with. They are concepts I have lived with and been guided by. I have a linear scale of values, to one end of which belongs Asat and to the other Sat. Yet now I am merging the whole span into one point which I determine totally as nothing but untruth. And at the same time, I retain the word Sat, Truth, for a transcendence, make that the goal and glory of all striving, and ask whatever presiding Benevolence there be to lead me from the present stagnation into that fulfillment. Obviously SAT has now to signify in lofty detachment a state far removed from that I had taken to be SAT in the relative frame of SAT-ASAT.

Similarly I admit in meek frustration that my known and lived Tamas, darkness or ignorance, has not been illumined by Jyothi, light or knowledge; that the words have pretended to signify two opposites whereas in reality they collapse into the nadir where only darkness prevails, and light from that source is an impossibility. Therefore what the mind sees as its knowledge, and its ignorance, are totally born of ignorance of Reality, which is Absolute Knowledge, and the mind can only function within relative knowledge. So, I pray for redemption, and in doing so, have no recourse but to signify the goal as Jyothi, returning to the word with new intent.

It is evident that there are pairs of words for the relativistic experience of all the values and perceptions of my sensed existence, and one is posited as a negative in opposition to the other which becomes the positive, but on close re-examination it turns out that both indicate one state only, and that is what had been termed as negative. Thus, mental truths stripped bare become falsehoods, and knowledge collapses into a heap of ignorance. Our sense of the positive emerges at best as a double-negative. Surely there must be more to positivity?

Coming closest to the core of my being, to LIFE itself which is the pre-requisite to discern existence or possess knowledge, I see it intimately in opposition to death. But on introspection my state is revealed to me to be the negation of the true significance of what life should be, and the prayer becomes a plea to be taken from Death to Immortality.

Strange, is it not, that I do not beseech my God to take me from life, which word should designate my present state, to Immortality, but I concede that my status now is death and pray that I may be led from this death to the positivity of LIFE eternal. We all know that from death the journey is to the cemetery! Therefore, in this prayer there is a reversal of meanings that were taken for granted for words of habitual usage, and the words have been transformed into winged vehicles of a voyage into transcendence. It is not a cry of despair, but a song of liberation. There is an exultant vision of personal potential that had for so long been obscured by a false but fatal surrender to limitation.

This then is my new conviction, that I am not the fragmented, time-bound individual I took myself to be. That is the history of the body and I have lamentably identified myself with this body, but in truth I am the consciousness energy operating through the body. I was Sat, existence, reality, before the body was fashioned out of elemental matter; I was Jyothi, light, knowledge, before the darkness, ignorance, possessed the ego-sense as the body of the person; I was the Life Eternal, Amrutham, before the temporal frame of flesh took birth to march to its death, Mruthyu.

How can the truth of Existence ever cease, how can the glow of Light be ever lost in darkness, how can Life be annihilated by Death? Is it not evident that the contrary alone occurs, that Existence denies and destroys non- existence, Light darkness, and Life death?

Naa Sato Vidyate bhaavo
Naa bhaavo vidyate sataha

– *GITA.II.16*

Of the non-existent there is no being.
Of the existent there is no ceasing to be.

And so, Oh Lord, this is my prayer to You: Take me from becomings to Being. Make me one with You. Now You are masquerading as many beings, and You make the eternal and total vibration of I, which is Your only sound and song, appear as though it is arising independently as the I-sense of isolated centres. I have taken myself to be one such centre, locating my I-ness as a thing apart and personal in my body frame. As long as the error remains undiscovered by my mind, I will continue to be a limited entity, interacting with other similar entities. The end of the body will neither eliminate me, nor enlighten me, as long as memories and desires perpetuate my ego-feel of myself, and I will seek change outside but not change myself inside. That would only mean a continuity of my ignorant state with its falsehood, darkness, death – Asat, Tamas, and Mruthyu.

So, my Lord, lead me out of this closed circle of error that imprisons me in relativity. Let me break out of it by Thy grace. You vouchsafed the Absolute to me. In my peevishness or perversity or poverty of feeling, I have so long denied it to myself, and preferred to believe conveniently that You denied it to me. Forgive me. Though I speak brave words now, the long-sustained false conviction that I was a cripple, has needlessly weakened my limbs. Take away my crutches. Hold me and lead me. Lead me to Immortality, the Home I was never asked to leave.

Part II

Contemplative

19
The Eternal Link

The compatibility of a Pure Being that is changeless and indivisible, with the ever-changing conglomerate of mind and matter that is creation, is the vexatious problem that Vedanta (the essential Hindu philosophic thought) resolves. It points out how the ignorance of Reality causes the false illusion, whereby Truth is not destroyed but only hidden. When all phenomena is brought to a focus in its origin, we are led to a concept of God (Paramatman) that can be rendered in terms of our understanding as Sat-Chit-Ananda (Existence-Knowledge-Bliss). Therefore Vedanta addresses Him as being of the Form (Swaroopa) of Sat-Chit-Ananda.

These three words are not only meaningful to our personal existence, pursuit, and purpose, but denote the three primordial and compulsive urges that energise life.

For all the veiling of ignorance, the glow is yet faintly visible, the glow that denotes His presence in me.

If instead of redeeming my lost heritage I halt on the wayside and demand that I be told then and there how there should have been at all the blemish of ignorance in Supreme Knowledge, Vedanta gives me the sufficient and not untrue answer that the delusion was caused by "Maya". "Aghatita ghatana pateeyasi maya" is the exclamation by the great master, Adi Sankara. It means that marvelous Maya renders the totally impossible as possible! It is like the mind creating by its own powers and content an unreal, but seemingly real, dream.

If I further protest "why did the good Lord have to do it all, even if He had the power of Maya to manipulate it?" Vedanta answers: "For His Leela," for His harmless playful indulgence. Only a petty mind, a mind that will not be awakened from the sleep of habit, will construe this negatively to mean that the miseries of the created are a cruel joke of an insensitive Creator. Its true purport is that agony is not an inescapable imposition inherent in a situation, but an infliction of an erring mind upon itself.

If with that we would stop questioning the motive and the method, and would resume the urgent quest for the Truth of oneself, these words would cease to be conundrums.

Man vaguely suspects under the promptings of a whispered instinct that he does not altogether cease to be from the moment of death. That is why there is a fear of death. We fear an experience that we anticipate. If there is to be no experience, where then is the need for fear, and for whom? The experiencer must be there. So when I think of my death, I am apt to wonder, "what will happen to me after I die?", and in thus wondering, I assert my deathlessness. Fear is always of the yet unknown that I will come to know hereafter. As death approaches, a decaying body may cause relentless pain, and one has to go through that pain. The recognition that the familiar will soon cease and the relating will soon end, may cause mental *suffering*, but fear is a thing apart, it is of an arriving uncertainty that will befall me – I will be there as the experiencer thereof. If I believe death to be a void that negates me, there may be a regret that experiencing will cease, but there can be no fear of an experience. The mind of man that fears the transition seems to possess an instinct that death is only a more pronounced change in life. Since life itself is never other than continuous change there can be no qualitative variation, and if what happens is only a quantitative change, there can be no death, ever! I who survive all the changes of life will live beyond the change called death that will end my use of this body-equipment. How is it that I am so sure of my undying existence, sure beyond reason? This is one question.

Life is an unending procession of thoughts. Thoughts cease only when one leaves the waking and the dream conditions, and enters into deep sleep. But in deep sleep the individual has no cognition of life at all. Nothing exists for him, nor does he exist as himself in his own awareness. To think of something, is to be conscious of the thought of that something. So life is one continuous experience of fragments of consciousness in the form of thoughts. Were it not so, neither do I myself exist, nor the world of my perceptions exists. Why is there this constantly pulsating experience of consciousness and how is it caused? This is the second question.

Every living being is forever seeking happiness. No one ever clings to a source of unhappiness, nor does one live in serene contentment saying, "I am complete in all respects. I need nothing that I do not now contain within myself". Hunger for food is one form of an inadequacy which life recognizes and seeks to remedy. Loneliness is another. Desire for wealth, for more possessions, is yet another. So is the egoistic urge to strive, to succeed, to excel. There is too the demand that comes from the secret recesses of memory for recall, remembrance, revival, so that the joy of a past moment does not perish. The individual becomes aware of a lack in himself which, if removed, he believes will render him complete. So he acts towards that end, achieves his objective, and momentarily knows happiness: but within an instant another incompleteness reveals itself and compels the mind's attention and redress. A thousand times, and a hundred thousand times, man attempts to become perfectly happy, but knows as often that he has chased a mirage. Yet he cannot stop trying. Whence this constant endeavour to be happy? How has man come to feel instinctively that he is incomplete, and that completeness will give him happiness, and that abiding happiness is what he wants for himself as the fulfillment of the entire process of life? This is the third and last question.

These are the questions into which are resolved all the doubt and distress and conflict and confusion of the human mind turning upon itself and seeing at once its irrefutable compulsions, its ceaseless exertions, its ordained limitations – in short, its agonizing tale of contradictions that can neither be endured nor ended. These questions are of course not posed by the insentient world, much less by an untroubled God, but by the aggrieved mind of man. And therefore the answers must be found in terms that the mind is accustomed to, and transacts in. The mind reasons that the world which is the cause of its experiences must have itself been caused, and caused by an Intelligence, caused for a purpose, for that is how it always is within the activity of the mind.

So Vedanta answers that the unitary Totality, indicated by the word Paramatman, can be seen by the focused mind as being at once of the nature of Sat (total existence) and Chit (total knowledge) and Ananda (total bliss). The homogeneous faculty of being aware of existence, of having knowledge, and of experiencing happiness, truly and exclusively belongs to Sat-Chit-Ananda Paramatman who is the only Experiencer. This of Him in the mind is the contact that seems to transfer the experience to the individual, making it both true and false at the same time.

The origin of creation in Paramatman is postulated as the emergence of Time-Space as a concept in the fathomless possibilities of His conceptualization. It is the first cause, the beginning of movement, the ripple that cannot find the farther shore on which to end itself. The indeterminate power in the Totality that made this possible can but be termed "Maya", and the inscrutable reason (if the mind insists on a reason) for the act can but be identified as "Leela".

As the one sun becomes a thousand suns reflected upon the tossing waters, as the one mind of the dreamer creates a mob of a thousand men veiling the singular truth, so He becomes the multitude of jeevas. And each jeeva thus inherits a touch of time, a trace of space, and a glimpse of reality. He who neither exists nor non-exists, who is neither eternal nor non-eternal, who neither knows nor knows not, permits the limited jeevas[1] to have at least the power to contemplate what can be comprehended, to indicate what cannot be known, to live as objective experience that which is in truth pure Subjectivity.

Thus the jeeva thinks of eternity in terms of time and yet interprets this idea with a freedom from time-concept. It is at once both courage and stupidity.

The courage stems from the concealed true nature, the stupidity from the veil of ignorance that covers the Truth. For, man, even as man, has not ceased to be Sat-Chit-Ananda swaroopa.

The SAT aspect of the Atman is what penetrates through the mask

1 Individuals, or sentient beings, each an ego-centre of consciousness.

and instinctively gives man his indelible concept of eternal existence, so that he sees not in the death of the body an end of himself.

The CHIT aspect of the Atman is what equates life with thought. The Mass of Consciousness (Pragnana Ghana) that is God, is reduced to its fragmentary and fleeting form of moded thought in the awareness of objectivity. And so man thinks, and thinks, and thinks. His continuing identity of himself is only this succession of related thoughts.

The ANANDA aspect of the Atman beckons to the confused mortal through all the layers of gloom and flickers in his concepts of happiness. Man is drawn unknowingly, but nevertheless unremittingly, towards his origin. Ignorance tempts him to attempt completeness by total acquisition, and fools him again and again. The method may be the cause of sorrow, but unerring instinct indicates the forgotten heritage and lays the compulsion.

And so at the core there is, even now and here, the fact of Sat-Chit-Ananda in each individual, in whatever state he may be. That is the link that was never broken, the salvation that was never denied, the perfection that was never removed, the light that was never extinguished. It is ever here, here even now, not a thing to be gained hereafter.

How beautiful, how heartening, how divinely merciful.

20
Vasana – Kshaya
(Beyond desire)

Today I have awakened to the recognition of a Higher Life, which is indicated as being incomparably superior to the attainments that life as I have been leading it can offer.

I have seen verbally that a mind in which the clamour of desires is silenced can come to know itself as the centre of universal consciousness, causing, controlling and circumscribing the whole movement of life. My memories of pleasure and pain mould my desires which dictate my attitudes and actions. They are my propensities, my Vasanas (or Samskaras) that make me the particular individual that I am. I now see that I can rise above the limitations of this individuality. Having convinced myself of it, and with faith in the correctness of my own logical evaluations, I have decided to follow the chosen path.

I have understood that my mind must be quietened and ultimately stilled into a transcendental Awareness, but between this knowing and the becoming lies, as a barrier, the sordid summation of aeons of existence. Intellectual appreciation of the futility of the past can only insure me against future follies but cannot instantaneously redeem.

This present and fleeting moment is yet a mighty monster, for it has been forged upon the anvil of Time by the entire past – or else it could not have been.

So today begins with a reservoir of past accumulations. My vasanas are a lake that must be drained through the sluice, and upon the bed of the dried lake shall be found the lustrous gem of my quest.

Two conditions are then necessary: Obviously, inflow of fresh waters must be prevented, or as a first step, minimised. Torrential streams pouring in their muddy waters faster than the restricted outset can drain them, must only result in the lake growing deeper and getting so sullied that whatever glimmer was reaching the surface from the luminous gem lying on the floor will henceforth be obscured.

Let me not expose myself to new experiences of sense gratification. Let me not search for fresh avenues of objective enjoyment. Doing only that which my recognition reveals to me as my bounden duty, as the residue from the past, let me remain for the rest withdrawn, quiet, silent. That is the prevention of fresh inflow. That much being accomplished, the other condition to drain the lake would be that the waters should be let out. And of course they should not flow back into the lake.

The import of Time in the scheme of creation must be unravelled. Time is subtler than the unvarying rotation of an inert globe round an unconcerned sun. Time stood with the whip of Will in hand and ordered the circus to start! How then can it be ordained by its mute creatures?

There is a meaning and a measure of time that cannot be reckoned by the lengthening shadows, or marked upon the dial of a watch. The sluice to drain the lake of Vasanas is Time. Avidya, (primordial ignorance of one's True Nature), the causal body, comes to be experienced as the subtle body through the medium of Time. The movement by which Cause becomes Effect is the hidden meaning of time. The dimensions of the sluice are indeterminate and varying. There are as many "times" as there are minds. The waters must be drained for each lake as the sluice permits. Of what use is it to wish that in one explosive outburst the lake may be rendered dry?

The waters will flow out and normally they will not return to the lake because they escape at a lower level and cannot flow to the higher banks unaided. So too will my Vasanas manifest as thoughts and actions, which cannot reverse themselves into the subtler substance of vasanas again, unaided. However, the escaping waters can be made to turn the wheels of a turbine and generate power, which can be employed to run a pump, which can lift the waters again and return them to the lake. A highly efficient device will lift back almost all the outflow, though to no sensible purpose!

We, ostensibly intelligent humans, are equipping ourselves with similar mechanism, which through the dedication of a perfect folly, has attained foolish perfection! It is the machine of Reaction.

Action is the expression of my personal equation at any given moment, an outward-bound movement from my mind, a natural quantitative deduction. But by reacting to the results of my action, either exulting in success or sulking in defeat, I reinstate in myself the causal seed for the same movement again and restore to the mind a burden that could have been discarded. Unnaturally, and indeed unnecessarily, we exert ourselves as stupidly as might a labourer digging a deep well if he were to struggle up the steps to the rim with head-loads of the loosened earth, only to dump them into the pit again.

When vasanas manifest as activity their bondage is more easily borne than when they manifest as memories only. In action itself there is a distraction, a fulfillment, a balancing of accounts. But when a mere memory, glad or sad, occupies the mind, the bondage is subtler. Let us beware, and not attempt to force forgetfulness, for forgetfulness cannot be forced. The very act will perpetuate that which it would presume to destroy. The method is to turn passive witness, to be aware of the returning memory without conflict or support, to let it remain without welcome or abuse.

Obviously the fruits of actions will carry within themselves the seeds that will sprout into trees of activity again. In our greed for the fruits we swallow them whole with the seeds! How can we avoid vaster activity rising from us?

Vasanas will end for me when I act because I must, and not because I will. Then the factual compulsions of a retained past fulfil themselves inexorably, but the action flows through me without my assumed doership. They will end when I am in no hurry to end them through denial, but am gladly prepared to bear the self-imposed yoke. They will end when I move in step with the ceaseless movement of Nature – when I am natural.

21
In Memoriam

A girl of ten, sweet and gentle, narrated to me this episode. We had been sitting under a mango tree and talking quietly. Then, unnoticed, the conversation had ceased and both of us had, by unspoken consent, preferred to watch the leaps and loops, the flutter and frolic of the creatures of the garden in the branches of the trees. When time moved again, I looked at her and saw in her eyes an urge to communicate. So, softly I said" Tell me," and this is what she said:

"A week ago, one day I was sitting in my room, perhaps reading a book, when I was startled by a sound, for the squeals that suddenly filled the air were unmistakably born of fear – which made me wonder later that a tender life so recently arrived upon the terrestrial scene should instinctively recognise danger and feel frightened – and I rushed out to find a baby squirrel, oh such a baby it was!, on the verge of falling prey to a carrion beak. With frantic motions and loud invectives I chased away the black murderer and sheltered the little trembling body in my palm. In the branches overhead two other crows settled down with a warm carcass in the claws of each. Only one had survived from the ill – fated brood of three little squirrels.

"Thus did Fluffy come into our lives, my brother's and mine. I remember what he said when I took Fluffy to him. He said an act of kindness was the truest form of prayer. He said perhaps I had then been nearer God than if I had spent a whole morning with folded hands. I thought so too.

"Fluffy was a grave responsibility. With a dropper we fed him with milk, which he swallowed contentedly, moving his little mouth the while, much as a child would. And then he slept peacefully in a nest formed in a small box with a silk scarf.

"Fluffy would wake us up with his early twitter. He was angry and as impatient as any hungry babe for the drops of milk.

"He brought gaiety to our home. He commanded attention from every member in the house and we were his loving attendants. He was growing rapidly and broke the silence of each successive dawn with increased vigour. His soft coat took on new lustre.

"For three days and three nights Fluffy was our pride and joy. On the fourth, when we relaxed our vigil for one fatal moment, he slipped out on to the grass outside to try his new-found strength in little gambols. The fate that he had escaped once was not to be denied a second time. In one heart-breaking flash a crow swooped on him and took him away. Fluffy's last squeals reached us for a few seconds... and then there was silence. Fluffy's feet had scampered on to the clouds and the sunshine beyond.

"Was God then not in His seat? Our knowledge is too little for us to judge, says my brother. But I am young and inexperienced and this act of divine justice I cannot understand. Is there in Heaven too revenge and retribution along with love and forgiveness? Do the young pay for the acts their fathers did? Are little squirrels created in all their glory to satiate the hunger of murderous beaks?

"I do not know. I only know that Fluffy was too young to die."

I let her sob a while. "You hate that crow?" I asked. "Yes, yes," she said.

"For killing the squirrel?" "Yes, of course."

"And you hate cats that kill mice?" "Yes" she said.

"And tigers that kill?" "Them too"

"If they didn't kill, how would they live? Each creature is living according to its nature. By your ideas of what is sinful, the crow becomes a criminal. But are you not wrong in judging another, be it a crow or a fellow-being, by your needs and your ideas of fair and foul?"

"But Fluffy was killed, finished off so young", she wailed.

"Child, God is wiser than we know, and creation is vaster than we can conceive. Death is not an end of Life, but a change in living. We fear death, for it is normal to fear the unknown, but fear through anticipation itself be-speaks a continuing presence, does it not? Ignorance remains with the survivors. Do not grieve long for any death. Life and death are both God's gifts. Do not take credit that you saved Fluffy. That too was His act. And the killing was His act too. For both He had His reasons. Why are you questioning the one and not the other?".

And then we talked of lighter things, for at ten tears are volatile, and soon she sprang up, smiled and ran away. I watched her go, smiling to myself; for had she not questioned creation, thereby taking the first step towards the understanding of the Creator?

22
Not To Question "Why"?

During serious discussions of a philosophic bent, it is sometimes said that "why" is a foolish or redundant question. Even to that statement, the mind's first reaction would be "why"? Let us examine the implications further.

The objection must be viewed dispassionately. "Why does it rain?" is admitted as a valid question. The reply may be: "Because of clouds that are laden with water." "Why are the clouds thus laden?" is again admitted. Let us say: "Because of the sun and the sea." Now how heat evaporates and cooling condenses are relevant to the enquiry, but "why should the sun be hot?" in the tenor of asking "why should there be a sun at all?", is a puerile wordy superfluity when one might as well save breath and come to the core-question that is implied in the extensions and will appear finally – why not sooner than later? – "why should there be phenomena? Nay, why should there be creation?" Now, the mind thinking on its own accustomed terms, equates existence with creation, posits a creator and endows him with intention – that is the only way the mind's script runs. So it harps on the question "why did God create?"

without the decency to be honest and first define the God whose motives it would aspire to decipher, and whose methodology it would unravel.

So, the question is turned back upon the questioner. If he would know why God created, let him tell who is the God he speaks of. Then when he pauses in confusion, the Master who at no time was joining issue with him, much less seeking to ridicule him, says with fond persuasiveness: "If God is unknown to you while you are known to yourself, before you ask "who is God?", ask 'who am I?'and reexamine critically the criteria you accepted so far to validate yourself."

In the process, the inadmissibility of "why?" as a primal question stands vindicated.

To the repeated question "why?" the repeated answer can only be "because". "Because" means be-cause, the cause being thus. When we ask "why is this so?" we are standing upon the threshold that is the effect, and looking backwards at the cause, that is, going from effect to cause. The flow of life is from cause to effect, not from effect to cause. But the mind of man has become involved in cause-hunting. It is for ever asking "Why, why?" This is basically a flow opposed to the natural current. No wonder then that there is so much of turbulence, the eddies of obstructed flow.

The present is the inevitable consequence of the past, the natural conclusion of everything that has preceded this moment, the manifestation of the total cause that has gone before. Since the serene and immutable law of causation is forever functioning, and forever the same, the present is the only possible summation or manifestation of the entire past. In that sense the present experience of the questioner has been willed by the past of the questioner himself. What answer can be made then to him that asks "why is this so?" except to say "because you willed it so, you who are the continuity of the past into this moment". And if that is the only answer to every question of "why so?" surely it is pointless to ask the question?

He who questions the phenomenon is in reality questioning the natural law. To the man of wisdom, this is a waste of time and energy. "How shall I deal with it?" or"what shall I do now?", would be the sensible approach. "Why?" takes one backwards, not forward. The law is not to be questioned, it is to be met by understanding, initiative, and relevant action.

If the mind is indulged and allowed to go backwards and yet backwards into the cause of things and events, it will ultimately have to ask "why was causation caused?". To say that the first cause came uncaused would be no answer to a mind bent on asking "why so"? At that stage, the mind has to be told: "The Reality in you is the Supreme Consciousness from which causation arose. So you yourself as the Totality caused the first cause. Become one with your True Nature, and answer the question to yourself. Supreme Consciousness or call it the Reality, your kinship with which cannot be annulled by the mere disadvantage of your forgetfulness, is free of the distorting association of Time, whereas you, being within time and therefore within the endless coils of causation, are inescapably conditioned by the change. The beginnings of causation cannot be found within the boundaries of the mind, nor can the mind transcend its temporal chains to touch timelessness. You are not the mind, its limitations are not yours. Break free of memory and experience the Truth of yourself." No other answer is comprehensive because the mind is, at that point, trying to see itself as it were, an attempt as impossible as that an eye should see itself.

To say this, is not to suggest that all enquiry into "why" should cease. The mind, whose highest attainment would be to move concurrently with steady-flowing Time, is caught up in its endless manoeuvres as it scurries now into the past, now into the future, restless and full of anxiety. If it cannot stop this movement altogether, atleast let it move with dignity and quiet purpose. Let it delve back into the causes, study them, analyse them, assess them, and emerging, use the knowledge to go firmly forward without looking back timidly over the shoulder at each step.

At least that much is possible for all of us. It would be a more dynamic and efficient way of conducting our affairs of the intellect. Knowing that cause-hunting is a retrograde step, whose gaze is directly opposed to the harmony of natural forces, can help us to have the correct perspective, which in turn can give us strength and a great purpose.

23
The True Leader

No man has done his best, except he that became a Jeevan-muktha.

Even in the fields of relative experience, those great men whom the world admires, whose selfless devotion to the service of humanity, and whose boundless love that seeks no return, are daily bringing blessings to the needy of this earth, will themselves readily concede that they could have done better. Horizons always recede when approached. Few in number are the men who even know the limits which man can reach. Those are the sages who transcend relativity.

Let us remember this, for we too have till now forgotten our potential. We have succumbed to the saving grace of the convenient conclusion that we have done our best, and somehow others have not measured up. Let us face the fact ... THERE CAN NEVER BE A CRISIS OF FOLLOWING. THERE CAN ONLY BE A CRISIS OF LEADERSHIP.

Let us be watchful lest escapism should put on the garb of humility, for when it parades thus, a dangerous situation is created. A leader has been entrusted with the task of leadership, only because the others credit him with possessing faculties they themselves lack. In accepting the assignment, the leader evidently concurs with the group's opinion that, all things considered, under existing circumstances, he is well suited in that group to show the path which all shall tread. Then, to put on an air of injured innocence and say "After all, who am I? I have humbly tried my best, but no one responds" – this surely, is hypocrisy? The heart of the matter is simply that such a leader did not come anywhere near doing the best that was projected as the possibility. If a leader has done his best, and it has been found that his best can be improved upon, let the criticism come from the group, for in the process, a better must be pointed out, or else the accusation is in vain. Meanwhile, the leader has no call to decry himself – let him engage in the positive and dynamic task of honestly doing his best.

Let me introspect, for where expect in subjective analysis can the answers be found? Let me gaze on my own personality honestly.

Having accepted an assignment as leader of a social cause, or as political crusader, or head of a commercial enterprise, or as a spiritual missionary, how earnestly have I given of my thought and time and energy to the cause I willingly inherited ?

How often have I evaded working with groups of my colleagues or assistants, even though I knew fully well that my presence would have pleased and encouraged those groups to function better ? A dozen excuses have readily offered themselves every time, and yet I was willing enough to put back a full day's work to respond to a friend's unexpected proposal of some merry-making. Selfishness masked duty.

Agreed that we are imperfect – or else where is the need to strive ?

Agreed that we have to learn, to know, and slowly to become. But if we lose sight of our true potential, if we delude ourselves into thinking that the end is within reach when we have but just turned our faces towards the destination, and worse still, if we look upon environments as deciding finalities, how shall we lay stake to our limitless heritage ?

Let, then, the leaders lead. Let them lead with confidence, and others will follow with faith. Let them strive with earnestness and conviction, and mountains will be dislodged. Let them sing with full-throated joy and even in the lonely wilderness, meek echoes shall form themselves into a repeating chorus.

The true leader is really the truest follower. The true master is really the truest servant. Therein lies the force that unifies. A true leader shall not lack a following, that is the law.

24
The Portals of Self-Enquiry

Tossed and tormented by the waves of hope and desire, that entice us as sunny ripples but change unknown into vicious breakers and transform the moment of frolic into the hour of despair, some of us somehow regain the tranquil shore, and begin to contemplate the occurrence in order to prevent a recurrence.

Such a one am I, and if such you too be, we will keep company through this page, or else we part here, to go each his way.

Tell me now, my friend that have chosen to stay with me, whether if in this instant a benevolent dispensation grants us the fulfillment of all the hopes earlier withheld, and all the desires earlier denied, our minds will know abiding peace? How long will it be before we are enmeshed again in demand and despair, in hope and fear?

When we see the banality of our method in seeking happiness through satiated desire, while in truth desire fuels further desire, a resentment of the travesty we have made of our lives so far is felt, and the mind withdraws into itself to consider with earnestness and urgency: What is my true nature? In what lies fulfillment? What, indeed, am I?

The enquiry looks critically at the concept I have had of myself, wherein I am this body solely or essentially. I may be accommodative and concede that I am this body with a special capability I recognize as consciousness or awareness or mind or life. With this faculty I am alive (a live body) and without it I am dead (a dead body). The unquestioned implication so far is that the special attribute of mind or life is a function of the body; that is, structured as it is, this conglomerate of insentient flesh, skin, bone, brain and blood, has biochemical capabilities to generate the energy that is experienced by itself as sentiency, or consciousness.

The contradiction between an insentient mass giving rise to sentiency now has to focus attention upon itself, till it is seen beyond further dispute that it cannot be thus. The energy of consciousness must be a self-existent and independent truth; energy is not produced (created) by matter, howsoever structured, but only manifests as a force that acts upon and moves matter. It follows that energy which exists independent of matter, and manifests its properties as a force when related to matter, cannot be destroyed when its association with material vestures is ended.

It further follows then that life in me, understood as the energy that manifests as consciousness or activity in me, cannot be destroyed by the phenomenon called death. My death can only signify that my life-energy (my mind – capability) can no longer manifest in that body, and lacking that support the body has turned into an insentient corpse. When the flow of electrical energy has been switched off, the moving (living) fan has become the still (dead) fan. But did electricity die?

This moves us to a perception of the subtler truth of oneself as the energy that abides in or constitutes one's mind, which is the totality, or else the essence, of its experiences, feelings, responses, memories. My mind is my own (as yours is yours) with its circumference of which I (my I-ness) am the centre, a circle that may expand or contract, but always a limited separate entity. So it seems.

Till again the enquiry, being earnest and urgent, reexamines the early acceptance of a life-time's habit, and arrives at the question, "What can limit consciousness? Make of it a fragmented entity?" My mind has to answer this question, and obviously any answer can only give verbal shape to what the mind perceives, and whatever is perceived is only a mode of consciousness, a thought within the mind. So it becomes akin to drawing a circle upon the sea with water to demarcate a small area of the sea! The mind can conceive of nothing that can be its container, for whatever is conceived is already its content!

The prompting of a totally new dimension to one's being (reality) is felt within the mind that has turned its gaze upon itself. I-ness is not circumscribed, it cannot be. When the frontiers of my mind are seen to be non-existent, its unbroken identity with the Total-Mind, the Total-Consciousness is sensed. If this body of mine was the limited equipment with which my limited mind identified, in the expanded reality of the total mind it is obvious that the whole universe constitutes its body-equipment.

Then there is in truth a unitary consciousness, expressing through a unitary equipment (universe), and the whole phenomenon is a unitary movement.

And you my friend, still by my side in shared discovery, are to me not other than me, as in another dream where I was the dreamer and you were my friend in the dream, we were both inherent in one dream-movement that arose in one dream-consciousness of one ME. In the restored reality of myself as the waking-I when the dream had ended, there was only one architect, one experiencer of the dream, he that could say: I dreamt, I was there, you were there, but in truth nothing was there. It seemed I was that one, but I am this one, and have never been other than this one. Do you see, my friend, that you cannot in the morning assert your presence in my dream of last night? And that therefore there is only one I into which all the 'me' and 'you' and 'they' and 'it' must resolve?

To have sensed that as the ultimate Truth of oneself is to have arrived at the portals of Self-Realization. It is the entrance through the arch upon which are inscribed the immortal words with which Bhagavan Ramana Maharshi launches the earnest seeker upon the final voyage of delight and discovery:

WHO AM I?

25
The Present In Time

What I do not perceive, does not exist for me. In fact it is redundant to say that it does not exist "for me", because then, for whom else does it exist ? To say that it exists for others is illogical, for in that case I should be aware of what it is that I am referring to, and in that very thought it would have become an object of my mental perception.

Therefore, the mind cannot conceive of existence without there having been a thought in the perceiver's mind of the existence of that object.

Now, the mind is a constant flow of thoughts. One by one my thoughts are known to me. There is a knower in me who stands still, and with reference to whom all thoughts pass by one after the other. Life at each instance is the experience of the fresh thought. The changing thoughts, however, give continuity to the occupation of thinking, and that is the whole of life.

The bank of a river never shifts, it is ever stationary. The water in the river is never stationary, it is always shifting. The flow of water makes what we call a river, the flow of thoughts makes what we call the mind. What is the bank that makes the flow of thoughts possible? It is the knower.

The immediate thought is the "present" in which the individual lives. Past and future are but thoughts of past and future, and the thoughts themselves are always the experience in the present. When viewed in this manner, time is but the fast renewed experience of the present; not something with a dimension extending unbroken from a beginingless past to a fathomless future, but rather a point that is everywhere and anywhere and always, and thereby acquires the semblance of dimension, as a fire-brand twirled fast creates the illusion of a ring of fire.

If there is no reality in our concept of the present, there can be no 'time' as we think of it, and hence no "creation".

Then, to know the present, to experience it in its very essence and being, would be to lay bare the mystery of Time and Creation. Can it be done?

The nearest I can come to the 'present' is to be aware of each thought as and when the Knower in me perceives the thought. But by then the thought has already been posited in front of the Knower, who remains changeless and motionless: that is to say, it is already an accomplished event, a thing of the past. It is significant that the word for it is a 'thought' and not a 'think'. The noun 'thought' is the same as the past tense of the verb form 'thought' and not present tense "think". (Strange how the English language stumbled upon the word so appropriately, though surely lacking the sanction of the logic that we are now dealing with!).

To borrow Swami Chinmayananda's calculated irreverence for

English grammar to emphasise the point, the thought has been 'thoughted' by the time I am aware of it! I cannot approach the origin of thought any nearer. I seem incapable of knowing the present as accurately or intimately as it must exist. All that I know of time and mind can only enable me to conclude that I cannot know the real present and so I cannot know Time, for, as was deduced earlier, Time exists as a dot in the microcosm of the present.

As the eye cannot see itself, the mind cannot know itself. The abstractions, for knowledge of which mind gropes in vain, must be what constitute the Mind itself, that being the reason why the Mind cannot know them. Time is only the Present in its abstraction, becoming in manifestation the measured time of our temporal reckoning. That Time, and Mind, are one and the same. They are the creative methodology of the cosmos. Individually, there are as many 'times' as there are 'minds'.

Between the ending of one thought and the rising of another must lie Time, the Present. That must be Silence, for thought is the first sound. That must be the Power, for all thought is created there. That must be the Force which sends forth helplessly all beings into creation, sustains them for the duration of thought, and redissolves them in the stillness of the trough between two waves. Macrocosmic time is measured in the Yugas; microcosmic time is in the singled thought. The consciousness that prevails between two Yugas is the same consciousness that prevails between two thoughts – it is the true Nature of Lord Krishna.

No wonder, when some one asked Bhagwan Ramana where he could find God, the great Maharshi said: "Look between two thoughts".

26
The Place of Man in Evolution

Contemplate the marvel, majesty, and multitude of Creation. Then add to that variety also what has been and ceased to be. How can we rest content in the belief that the individual being enters this limitless arena in one puny role, for one instant of time, has its piteous share of experiences, and goes forevermore to its unspecified end? Would even that mortal magician of modern America have created his famed Disneyland merely to take a child by the hand to allow it to stand for one moment at one of the entrances, only to be carried away at once with no hope of return?

Is Time then the sole spectator of this extravaganza of infinite creation, blind mute unconcerned Time with its mechanical movement, perhaps frightened of its own face? And if that be so, is not Chance the Creator and Probability the Providence?

There are those that would have us accept that life is an effervescence within the insentient matter that is structured into a body, that it is the secret chemistry of the intricate mix of minerals constituted as bone and brain, flesh and blood. Consequently, they say, life is coexistent and coterminal with the body. The individual spends its span of existence in seeking fulfillment of urges and desires born of its compulsions or volitions, which calls for struggle, defiance, adaptation. The scars of a lifetime are left in the mutations of body cells and become the inheritance of the body they reproduce. The nascent life-energy thus created starts its journey with advantage at the new frontier, and moves into its own struggle. There is no continuity of experience, they insist, asserting that the experiencing consciousness cannot survive the death of the body-equipment. As bees are robbed of their honey, are beings robbed of the fruits of their toil? When evolution prospers upon the sacrifices of the disowned predecessor, there is no grace in the giving and no gratitude in the gaining, there is only the tyranny of an eternity against an instant, and the success of a gust of wind that would aspire to weather the mountain face.

Thus would the scientist lock flashes of sentience in forms of insentient matter and make the totality of Life no more than a strand of beads strung on the thread of Time – to adorn a void? All else, he asserts, is idle speculation.

The seeker is too earnest to be interested in speculation. He focuses all his energy on looking intently at experience to see clearly the nuances of the basic fact of one's own existence here and now. This then is the true method of intelligence, not to ask for proofs of what it does not know, but to re-examine what it has taken to be the proofs of what it knows.

So, "what after death?" is not the question, but "what is life in me now?".

Life is an energy of mentation that expresses through body equipment even as electricity expresses as light through a bulb. Life is a force that moves matter, pervading it from outside, sufficient unto itself for existence but dependent upon matter-vestures for manifestation. The laws of any energy contain the factors and the equations that determine its expressions in related equipments, but the "death" or destruction of the equipment does not – how can it? – destroy the energy which merely continues to exist in its unmanifested state.

So life is indestructible. It continues in time. Truly, time continues only because life does so, and at life's behest. Without me, the cognizer, what is time?

Life is the cause of movement. Nay, living is movement. The urge for expression is sensed as desire, shaped as will, executed as action, and witnessed as change. The earliest forms that were thrilled by the touch of life ended an eternity of stillness with the magic and explosive joy of sentient movement, in itself a mighty freedom beyond compare, to be saved and savoured for a millennium. But no desire is the last...

Thus in the plant kingdom, how delightful must have seemed just the capacity to grow, even though the movement of growth could only be torturously slow. ..till with the passage of centuries of aeons, the limited freedom could no longer please, this standing rooted and imprisoned could no more be endured, the urge to move across and meet the neighbour could never again be suffered in meek bondage. And when the revolt was strong enough, the impossible of yesterday retreating to become the newly possible, and life in one rush of joy and abandon fashioning for itself a new body-form capable of yielding the fresh experiences ...worms proudly conscious of their conquest of space, mightier in achievement than the still-rooted oak, moving and meeting and mating...lost contentedly in a perfect world.

But for how long? Soon, once again, the pulling at the heartstrings, the inadequacy of moving but inches, the helplessness in wind and water, the desperate struggle before drowning in puddles, the mounting revolt whose other name is Will.

Till lo and behold, the impossible must become possible, the new experience must be grasped, and so the new form must emerge.

And now the mind, in the body of a fish, plunges and splashes, laughter in the heart, twists and turns and cleaves the conquered waters to establish mastery, and is content again.

Time waits. Time has time to wait!

The playful fish leaping through sunshine thrills to the motion of its body through weightless air, and muses idly upon the joy of soaring through outward space. The thought returns, and returns, and returns ....and it is no longer an idle musing, but a revolution in ferment. Meanwhile, the small fish that would escape from the larger killer that chases it through the water, jumps into the air in one frenzied but futile effort, and dies wishing with all its being that it had the capacity to be airborne.

"If wishes were horses, beggars would be riders", says a cynic. Correctly, if wishes were intense enough, beggars could become emperors.

Thus, a new frontier in freedom, the bird upon the wing, seeking escape from this earth in dizzying flights, evolving fantastic capabilities of endurance and direction as in species that migrate, indulging in new faculties, happily the conqueror of the elements!

Happiness? Peace? Can the mind have them? Can it be life's purpose to conquer the elements?

Lo, the bird no longer wants its wings!! I have scanned the horizons only to return to my nest, it says. I have left the earth only to seek its protection at last. If I have wings, I cannot desist from flying, and I no longer want to fly.

Then, be a fish again? No, the fish must fly to evolve and the bird must seek a new, new form that is neither fish nor bird, in which the urges of both are transcended.

The animal world is born; forms to suit the mental moods, changing when change is demanded imperiously, irresistibly, imminently Living by size, living by strength, living by cruelty, or else by meekness, living by guile. World after world of perception, mind tenanting that equipment which can serve the mood; placing itself in that environment which can provide the needed reaction, matter and mind functioning subject to one immutable, serene, unconcerned law of gravitation that eternally moves existence to experience ...what but this did our ancients call "Karma"!

Until at last, what avail these freedoms, these frolics, these fleeting fancies? I am weary, cries the mind, and lonely, and lost. I have conquered and possessed and played, and yet all that remains is a sad emptiness.'I cannot save myself. Save me, oh... oh... Unknown!

In that recognition of one as yet unknown and unnamed who shall save, is born Man. The mind that attained supremacy over wave and wind, that killed relentlessly or stood unmoving through ages, now no longer reaches out for physical freedoms or bodily endurance. The mood has changed completely. Fin and wing are instinctively known to be impediments and not aids; it will have no more to do with them. The equipment is no longer intended as an instrument of achievement in itself. The mind has begun to suspect that freedom cannot be perfected through widening experience. Liberation lies beyond activity, beyond structuring. For this final attempt and attainment, the mind fashions the body of Man to serve the heightened intellect.

Wherefore shall this biped grow wings again, or race the wild wind, cleave the waters, or see what lies beyond the horizon? Millenniums have taught him that the path of progress lies not in physical mastery over matter. The past is contained in the present, and needs not the sanction of memory to be so.

The most balanced instrument has been developed. The lighted lamp has been moved from field to field, and many are the spectacles that have been witnessed. What colours, shapes, and sizes! What a parade of feelings! What fantasy of thrills and terrors! Soon now the flame of the wick will falter and fade with a farewell flicker into the Eternal Dawn. If one chooses to bend a last glance back – wards from the threshold of Life Ever-lasting, what a mysterious mythical mischievous panorama will be revealed!

Man is not the final product of evolution. Man is all of evolution.

27
The Healing Touch

(At the inauguration of a hospital for serving the poor amongst us)

"Sacrifice is charity done by a bankrupt on unsuccessful borrowing".

Someone said that. I quote from uncertain memory, but I relish the content. I like its sledgehammer sarcasm that shatters complacency.

I delude myself into believing that I have the choice – to act one way and please myself, or act another way and please someone else. I like to flatter myself that I set aside my natural and personally satisfying inclinations, to assume the role of one who will serve mankind. And this shift from what I would rather be to what I compel myself to be, I call sacrifice and deem it a virtue. The attitude should at best qualify me to be a paid welfare worker, on a monthly salary!

The pursuit of happiness and the avoidance of sorrow are the twin urges governing life in all its variations. This admits of no exception and is not subject to personal propensities. There is choice in the identity of what is happiness to each one, but from the compulsive urge to abide in happiness there is no escape.

Progressing thus upon the path of endeavour, I repeatedly arrive at the fork where one way is the continuity of direction, while the other is a digression. Shall I spend this sum of money, which is now mine to spend, on a holiday for myself, or shall I use it to help some poor children through school? I know that a holiday in the hills is pleasurable and the vivid memory of a past year beckons gleefully. Yet if I decide to give in charity, it is only because my mind, as it is constituted, is capable of deriving a greater happiness from the deed, is seeing a higher fulfillment in foregoing for oneself and giving to another. It is identifying as a nobler value the choice that the indulgence of my pampered self shall yield to the basic needs of the less fortunate. And this mind of mine is surveying in one glance the alternatives that are no alternatives indeed, for already the lesser joy has turned to dismay in comparison with the larger, has it not?

So the inevitable thrust of life's law directs the current of my becomings on a course that cannot be denied. Of the real freedom to act to the contrary, I am bankrupt. Each one lives alone in the seclusion of experience within, and any expectation that what is not inherent can be borrowed from the external is a figment of imagination. Thus being a pauper, who cannot even borrow, shall I pretend that I am capable of doing charity; that I am truly endowed with the power to absorb sorrow into my soul thereby generating happiness in the souls of others? Shall I believe in sacrifice as a blessing that is born of suffering? That seed cannot be suffering, its true name has to be happiness.

Enough of it. Let us rise upon the soaring revelations of Vedanta, which are not words to hear, but truths to live by. All, all is for the Self, for there is naught besides the Self. So talk not idly of sacrifice. Talk, instead, of love, of identity, of unity. The hand does not serve the mouth when it feeds, and the nose claims no sacrifice in its sleepless toil of breathing for the sustenance of the body. Where oneness is experienced, therein is harmony, achievement, and fulfillment.

In this, then, must our hospitals be a dedication to our ancient culture and spiritual tradition. Not here shall one creed be praised through maligning another. Not here the invidious sale of a stale and sickly faith to a pain-racked passionless body. Not here the daily tally of a bank-balance wherewith to buy a berth in indulgent heavens, desiring that every embrace grudgingly banished on earth may be repaid a hundred-fold, and forever in an imagined heaven!

Here, we will say instead: "The Self in me is the Self everywhere. Though I have heard this, and comprehend its truth with my mind, I cannot feel the pain and agony of the sick, the needy, the bereaved. Oh Lord, save me from the banality of words, words, words. You alone have come to me in this form of a patient. You have given me this chance to feel, to love, to unite. I must see You in all these forms, serve You in all these forms. I must know that "I am all these bodies," before I can come to experience "I am not the body." Dear God, no one can love You that cannot love his fellow-beings. Unworthy as I am, You love me already, else You would not have blessed me with this opportunity. I cannot betray Your faith in me."

Words again ... But will they remain just words? Or, will they burn their impress upon our hearts? Bloom forth into acts of service? Time holds the answer in her folds and will not tell. Not yet...

But this we know. Our recent history has been the tragic tale of our imperfect devotion to a perfect ideal failing to achieve a tenth of what perfect devotion to imperfect ideals has achieved in the case of other creeds.

What avails the glory of Vedanta, the spherical perfection of Hindu thought? Today the infinite potential lies covered under the veils of our ignorance or indifference. Deliberate and conscious effort is necessary to regain for ourselves the inspiration that moved our forefathers. We have to create for our own evolution venues of service, and cleanse ourselves through dynamic activity whose only aim should be the expression of the essential unity in creation.

Few fields can offer the scope for it that tending the sick can. But it is not the drugs that count, nor the latest techniques, nor thy consummate skill in the arts of healing. The need is for the heart that can weep for a sorrow not its own. Such a heart once beat in a Gautama – and lo! The brief moment that witnessed the power of pure love has become an eternity. Centuries have not dimmed its lustre and noble hearts still discern in themselves the reflection of that light of compassion.

Let us take our artless love to these institutions – and humbly offer it to those that will bless us by acceptance. And when the balance is struck, we shall know that there never was a giving – only a receiving.

28
MAN IS THE PROBLEM

WHO would willingly "bear the slings and arrows of outrageous fortune"? We suffer them as the impositions of a merciless tyranny. Grudgingly we face life, which we declare is full of "problems".

What, may we ask, is a problem?

As long as your desires are being fulfilled, your wants satisfied, and nothing is contrary to your own wishes, there is no problem. But when your gratification is denied, your pursuit is foiled, the fruit you wish to enjoy is plucked from your outstretched fingers or placed altogether beyond your reach, that is a problem.

Have you stopped to ask by what supreme decree and what rights of inheritance you decided before the event that the result shall be as you would have it, that you alone shall be the favoured one? For all your moral posture and injured innocence, you are in truth demanding that the outcome, at a given point of time in a continuous movement, should be in accordance with your choice, regardless of all other factors that are a part of the movement and therefore influence the outcome and partake of it.

You live as one individual in a vast arena teaming with others like yourself, each one a centre of desires, ambitions and hopes that shape the aspirations and activity emanating from that centre. In this movement of the energy of life, as indeed in the operation of any insentient energy too, cause-effect relationship determines the resultant. As the cause, so the effect. There can be no effect that is not derived naturally from the operative cause. Since the potential causes its own effect, there is in the effect the truth and rightness of its linked continuity. How can that manifested effect be different at this moment from what the unmanifested cause held, any more than a plant can be different from its seed?

Thus are we all the prisoners of our own personalities, expressing in the present the condensed truth of the life each one has lived so far, his and her desires shaped by what one has enjoyed or suffered, exulted in or endured, through life till this moment. It is this truth of our past that projects us presently into the world to seek therein happiness in terms of our personal equations.

Just as you strive and crave, it is natural that every one else too is interested in the fruits of action. The resultant of the total action is the vector of the overall dynamics constituted of all the different contributions made by the participants. No factor is exaggerated and no factor is mitigated, each has its proper emphasis, no more and no less. In this resolution there is total justice to all, and no favour or prejudice to anyone. It is as it should be in terms of a perfect law, the cosmic law of causation.

When the resultant is thus manifested, who is to say that it is a problem, meaning it is not as it should have been? You say it, and in so saying, betray an enormous depravity of logic and reason. You want an effect that belies the cause. The problem lies only in your thinking that such violation of natural law is possible or preferable. Then obviously there is no problem in manifestation, there is only a problem in perception.

Since the sorrows and suffering of mankind arise from such misapprehension of truth, it has to be stated that *MAN HAS NO PROBLEM, MAN IS HIMSELF THE PROBLEM.* It is the mind which refuses to harmonize with the cardinal law of its operation that courts misery without understanding and suffers needlessly. The *desiring* mind must be able to see what it *deserves* too in the unbroken continuity of the movement of which it is an integral part, and not set itself up in futile conflict with the honest flow of cause into effect.

One who is obliged to traverse a terrain that is thickly strewn with thorns need not clean up the whole area to be able to walk across it, but by the simple expedient of protecting one's feet with sandals can step ahead without any impediment. So too can the individual that is clad with this perception go through life vigorously and joyfully, eking out of it everything that is one's due. The armour needed is the clear perception of the law of causation that in its totality is what KARMA signifies.

The law is seen as gravity when it works on matter and regulates the universal configuration of created mass. The solar system and all the galaxies remain the way they are because the law of gravity determines their respective locations and movements, equating effects with causes. Neither the insentient worlds of matter, nor the mechanical law of gravity, know themselves or one another. Where knowing is not, there is no recognition of anything, neither problem nor fulfillment.

The same law works on mind too, mind which is a configuration of thoughts, a movement in consciousness. The law works here too with the same rightness and rigidity, but here the individual mind sets itself in opposition to the total mind, creates an eddy in the smooth flow of the current, calls this self-created disturbance a 'problem', and commiserates with itself. When the law is applied to the workings of consciousness it is more specifically called Karma.

The ego-centered individual, taking himself to be the embodied person, seeking abiding happiness in relationships and possessions, never questions the basic premise of his methodology and therefore continues upon the erroneous path. He foolishly persists with the belief that his desire-motivated energies will bring to him the happiness and peace that he craves for. He needs to learn that the fruits of work are determined by the ordained operation of one eternal law, which has no option but to run true to itself.

The law has not, and cannot have, the vagaries of chance in its working. If it has, it will not be a law. There is the consistent principle of Intelligence behind it, for it is the decree that is the self-expression of the Absolute as the Uncaused-cause (as it were), setting in motion all the becomings of manifestation.

Bhagavan Ramana Maharshi gives us the supreme teaching in His UPADESA SARAM. At the very start He says the law of becomings is *kartuh (the Lord's) Ajna* (ordainment). It is not a small thing, not a casual or insignificant thing, it possesses the mighty authority of His sanction. But, note this too. *Karma tat jadam,* the law is insentient, it can only run the stipulated course and never waver. What note can it take of anyone's pleadings?

Should not I, the conscious entity, relate to the Law-Giver who is Total Supreme Consciousness and find my unqualified identity there through the right appreciation of the identity that already exists as an I-centre, instead of holding out suppliant hands to insentient *(jada)* karma, and remaining miserable that "problems" were not redressed? WHO AM I? Earnest pursuit of the question lifts the deluded *"victim"* of karmic manipulations into the seat of LORDSHIP over Karma.

29
Watch That Train

(The scene is set in rural India of past decades when steam-powered locomotive engines hauled loaded wagons or carriages across the country's vast stretches).

The villager, bless his simple soul, gazes in wide-eyed wonderment as the old railway train with its steam – engine thunders past his fields furiously, as compared with the of his cherished bullock-cart. He says to himself:

The boxes (carriages) are pushing this thing along. They are propelling ahead of them the funny carriage (engine) which they push firmly ahead of themselves. This carriage is cute, but rather silly with its puffing and huffing. Because its body is pushed, its wheels are turning, and they have tied the wheels together with a bar – rather pointless, if you ask me. But then, you would have thought they would stop at that, and be more adult than to connect that bar to something (piston) that constantly runs in and out, of a closed box (cylinder)! If ever there was a purposeless contraption, this last one is surely it...

And, with this soliloquy and a derisive nod and a knowing smile, he turns his mind to the plough and the land. He clicks his tongue and twists the tails of his team of oxen. The sun lingers poised above the hill-rimmed horizon as time stops awhile, and beholds again the ageless spectacle of the tiller at his toil...

How could the villager know that in his ignorance, he had turned topsy-turvy the logic of motion and motive-force, of cause and effect? That the closed box was the centre, wherein was generated the power that thrust the piston that turned the wheels that speeded the engine which dragged along the entire train of carriages?

Yes, how could the poor villager know, when so many intellectuals of our day are no wiser? For they will credit the world of objects with a will and volition, they will surrender to environment a sovereignty to which it is an impostor, and make of themselves victims and slaves, speaking pious platitudes about destiny. Wake up, oh misguided mortal: between the Karmic Law of Vedanta and your puny talk of "destiny" lie an ocean of ignorance and a mountain of endeavour. We will talk of higher matters when we rise to higher levels, but now bestir yourself and experience the power and freedom that your own will and your discriminative faculty can offer you.

So see first that you are the engine, taking with you, by your will and wish, the long train of worldly perceptions and memories.

Your body is moving along, and the organs of action are functioning, because you are motivated by the mind. The mind is the set of wheels on which the engine goes forward.

Yet you are apt to attribute to the construction of the cells in the brain the origin of thought, making mind a product of matter. Remember the vil1ager's conclusion that the wheels of the leading engine-body were rolling because the carriages behind were pushing it?

The bar that ties the wheels is moving not because the wheels are rolling, but on the contrary, the wheels are being turned by the tie-bar. In you, the bar is the Ego that links the various aspects of the mind, and gives them motion and harmony and continuity.

Rising and falling at a rapid pace, the Ego sets the wheels of sense perceptions in constant revolution, which results in desire-prompted bodily activity amongst sense objects.

Yes, the villager laughed at the cylinder. Totally unnecessary, he said. An appendage, an impediment, a superfluity. Similarly do our intellectuals discard with arrogant assertion the God that the humbler ones amongst us concede. In the cylinder is generated the power that pushes the rod that turns the wheels that carry the engine that drags the train. There is the essence of the matter, the focal point of power, the sequence of action and the very purpose of it all. So too, there is an Awareness, a Power, a Will that gives sentiency to the Ego whose motion causes all other activity in the individual.

One should have the earnestness to contemplate and the courage to question how insentient matter, extracted from food and constituted as the body of flesh and bone and blood, *could be the originator of life and of the conscious self- assertion of being and knowing;* how energy which functions through matched equipment could be mistaken to be inherent in, and therefore alone expressing through that matter equipment. A mental concept of God by harassed humanity would be no closer to fact than an assumption that the first one amongst the train of carriages had some- how a preferred function! The Truth of God has to be ascertained in the culminating experience of a vigilant mind that will see the cause behind the effect, the energy behind the motion, the Life-principle behind sentiency.

But there are those that would deny this, that would proclaim self-sufficiency unto the body and make God no more than a concept of an escapist mind.

To such, we can only say: "Go, stand by the villager and watch the carriages push the engine whose wheels make one end of a rod go meaninglessly in and out of a static cylinder," for how shall we tell them that upon the twin rails of Time and Space, mind hauls memory along, powered by Consciousness?

30
Prarabdha and Purushartha (Fate and Free-Will)

During enquiry, the question may arise: "Is Prarabdha greater than Purushartha, or is Purushartha greater than Prarabdha?". The same question is phrased differently when the troubled seeker asks: "Fate or free-will? Which of these signifies the course or control of my life?" In the early stages of our spiritual evolution, it behoves us to bclicvc that Purushartha is greater, so that we may have hold of an operational principle for daily activity.

Prarabdha-karma is then interpreted for the disciple as the causal flow that, at the given instant, is manifesting. We know that cause cannot be perceived except as effect. Energy is never perceived as such, but only in the effect it brings out. Electricity in the abstract is not seen and known, it is experienced as light in the bulb, motion in the fan, or heat in the heater. From the effect we deduce that the related appropriate adequate cause must have been there prior to the manifestation. The result produced when the cause is transformed into effect, in the rightful timing ofthe laws of energy flow, is obviously choiceless, even as the plant and flower and fruit that time brings out from a seed can be none else than what is decreed by Nature already nestling in that seed. That emergence, revealed moment by moment, is Prarabdha. It cannot but be that presentation, and that alone, at that instant. We can have no quarrel with that. If we have, we stand over-ruled.

Purushartha, the disciple is told, is how you deal with the Prarabdha that confronts you. What confronts you is not within your present will to choose, but how you deal with it is open to choice and variations within the limits of your personal competence. You can will your response in meeting the situation. Your mind can structure the alternatives of your reaction, your intellect can determine the chosen course, and your will can act on it.

Thus in your inherent strengths you can rise above Prarabdha and remain master of yourself. This is the free-will in the operation of Karma, the dominant freedom. But with freedom, there has to be responsibility. As you will, so you act. As you act, so you become. You are responsible for what you are at this moment because you have willed yourself into this present person, and you remain answerable to yourself in future which shall be the true and fair result of how you exercise your will henceforth.

The confidence that upon our own will and effort will depend our achievement and progress, is necessary to rouse us, from thoughtless tamasic surrendering to a sense of doom, into rajasic dynamism, and to spur us to incessant effort to attain a well-defined goal.

However, when at a higher level of seeking, the mind returns to the same question as to which of the two is greater, the Guru says "To whom are Prarabdha and Purushartha? Let him to whom both refer answer which is the greater".

On being prompted and provoked thus, we think afresh, and we come to see that if Prarabdha is the outcome of one's vasanas (that is propensities) so is Purushartha too the outcome of one's vasanas, and the resultant of the inter- action of the two is also the expression of vasanas. Within this homogeneous mass of vasanas, which are accumulated and congealed tendencies, divisions seem as futile and fleeting as lines drawn upon water to demarcate distinct areas.

The continuity of experience which has resulted in bringing about the specific Prarabdha-Karma that has now manifested as my experience, is the same causal structure that instructs and energizes my free-will at this moment. They constitute one homogenous factor and are not two independent disconnected factors. The determination of cause-effect sequence includes what the mind faces, as well as how it responds, for both the sensing and the reacting refer to the same mind and there is nothing external.

Then again, the Purushartha of one instant is part of the Prarabdha in the next instant, because it is potential cause that turns into manifested effect, and that effect itself is forthwith the cause for the next effect. The tree causes the seed which then causes the tree. In this consistent flow, which is cause and which is effect? What divides them?

They may be spoken of as two sides of a coin which has no thickness. Yet something divides them. The mind is always recognizing two aspects of Causation, the cause aspect and the effect aspect. What is it that divides them?

To understand our present state and the modalities of our mental conditioning, we must try to postulate rationally the beginnings of mentation. To us, consciousness is a flow of thoughts, it is a process of change and movement. So at the source of this movement we postulate a still and motionless Total Consciousness. That would be our projected determining of the Original Absolute Being, or Brahman or God, and from that Potential Source we have to derive the methodology of its transformation into Kinetic Energy which we experience as mind in motion. Such an enquiry must reveal the self-contained answer that Space and Time are the primal concepts to support objectivity; for, any object must rest in space at some point of time. Then subject-object relationship gets launched, and that is the content of knowing and sensing and experiencing. That is the mind, the ceaseless flow of thoughts.

It follows then that conceptional Time-Space becoming potentialized in unitary Total Consciousness is the beginning of division into plurality. And in the play of the many, the limited ego-sense of the person divides the one stream into two, positing itself as the independent doer (subject), and the rest as karmic compulsion. This erroneous conviction has subjugated the mind of man.

See simply and clearly what space and time mean to you and me in experiential terms. Space is the interval between two objects which have their independent existence apart. Between them is space. Between you and me, between you and the tree, between me and the cloud, we become aware of space. Thus space is a measurable perception, a linear reality to the mind. Similarly, time is an interval between events (or happenings). Between your arrival and departure, between sun-rise and sun-set, be it even between lightning flashing and ceasing, there comes to the mind the awareness of time as an interval, again a linear measure. But to you and me, space-time that is non-linear, a dimensionless existence, is inconceivable. Yet conceptual non-linear Space-Time must have its validity in Total Consciousness.

You and I are unable to deny and go beyond our current distorted experience of created space and time because your and my ego-sense (our I-ness) was itself not present at the Source. The personal ego arose mid-stream as part of the subject-object relativity and cannot disengage itself. Such a disengagement would have to mean the destruction of relativity, and nothing less. That in turn would mean the end of space and time as the links of continuity. In terms of our mind and its awareness of existence, we would have to say it would be a timeless state. What would happen to my ego then?

The goal of the seeker is to eliminate thought-flow, and make the mind still. The ego, with its accent on self-perpetuation, recoils in apprehension from the thought of thoughtlessness, seeing it as a void, nescience, negation. It is there that the right instruction and illumination can be drawn from the distinction we have already made between conceptual Space-Time in Total Consciousness which is the Creator's Freedom, and the experiential space-time which is the ego's bondage. Then will dawn the realization that the end of the ego-I by transcending the space-time myth is not death, but Life-Eternal, the awakening of I-I-I (as Bhagavan Ramana Maharshi has persistently taught us), the truth of the unbroken unchanging Being.

Therefore it is important for the seeker to analyse the concepts of time and space and carefully establish his relationship with them in their manifested state and in their abstract state. The freedom that flows from such right understanding is at once freedom from both Prarabdha and Purushartha.

31
The Seeker and Ashta-Graha Kutam

In 1962, the planets (Graha) of our Solar system, sailing through the skies in their ordained orbits, were due, in accordance with their inescapable geometry, to be so positioned that as many as eight (Ashta) of them would form a rare spatial cluster (Kutam). This occurrence, it was predicted, would bring dire disaster to our earth. The eminent astrologers and pandits of prophesy spoke in awed tones of the calamity soon to descend upon the human race.

Round the world there was fear, frenzy, caution; or ridicule, bravado, amusement.

The dreaded hour of doom arrived and departed without distinguishing itself!

Many prayed openly. Many more perhaps prayed hiding their faces in their hearts.

This article was written then – in 1962.

The dreaded days of Ashta-graha assemblage have come and gone, and a world that held its breath in painful suspense now gazes around in bewildered relief. ”Nothing happened” everyone says, rubbing disbelieving eyes!

Yet, who is to tell that nothing happened? What if in the heads and hearts of millions new thoughts have rippled through during that period leaving an impress that will bear global fruit in the future? Then, would it not have been even more real and more potent a happening? Thoughts are the seeds from which actions grow. The atom-bomb exploded in the mind of a scientist long before it rained death over Hiroshima, but on the day the sinister secret revealed itself in a searching intellect, the people of Hiroshima would have said piously “Nothing happened today”.

So too with the days that saw the historic phenomenon of eight planets sharing for a brief length of time a limited segment of space. In silent obeisance to the immutable law of creation that fashioned in identical structures the microcosmic atom and the macrocosmic universe, the planets moved as they must, the law of probability merely expressed the odds on consequences, while the grand old sire Time nodded assent, the laws of gravitation functioned unconcerned with what mortals on earth thought or spoke, and the event occurred and receded towards retreating horizons. What did it all mean to us, and what should it have meant?

Let us begin by understanding what Astrology is, and what authority it possesses. Astrology is a codification of observed phenomenon, from which by the laws of precedent and probability a certain rationale is deduced, and thereafter it is the normal expectation that a given arrangement of the constellations will witness a given set of conditions upon the earth. The forecasts are derived from intricate equations of a multitude of pulls and pushes of mighty masses afloat in silent spaces, of worlds gyrating in an ocean of gravity, and the vectors of energies thus set in motion leaving their impress upon the prevailing equilibrium of the mind of mankind; for, in the ultimate analysis, mind, which is the subtlest aspect of matter, inevitably heeds the same laws. But this is only true of the mechanical mind that perceives and records. It is not true of the Intelligence that pervades and possesses the mind and uses the mind's subordinate functions in the freedom of its Will.

This is also the case with palmistry. If a hundred thousand palms are scrutinized, and the known characteristics of those hundred thousand persons are also studied, similarities, common trends, associations between line and mind, can be carefully compiled and compared. Soon a rationale emerges and the palmist can apply the documented rationale of the visible lines to the invisible character, when a fairly correct "prediction" is possible. The 'prediction' is really not other than a statement of the "probability".

Eminent astrologers assert that astrology is not deterministic, it is indicative. They point out that it is exactly because of this – the fact that predictions are probabilistic and not pre-determined certainties – that astrology is useful to mankind in the conduct of lives.

Laws of nature are neither malevolent nor benevolent. They run infallibly through eternity, unconcerned because laws are insentient. And matter submits to force as the law decrees, unperturbed because it too is insentient. But when the feeling, responding, willing consciousness of a person enters the equation, a totally different dimension is brought in. No phenomenon can determine or dictate the response of observer to occurrence. What indeed can any longer be doom to one that has unveiled Time and called the bluff of Death?

There were those who engaged their minds in the pursuit of this finite and not infallible logic, and predicted dire disasters or rate blessings. But why should a true seeker of Truth engage his mind in trying to know the future? Try as you will, you must live in the present, there is no other way. In the present you can think, if you so desire of the unmanifested time which is the future, or you can utilize the present to contemplate the Reality in what is being manifest here and now. The present is available for the enquiry "Who am I? What is the Self?" Whatever happens to me? Who is this ME? If I am the knower, what is the difference to me whatever is presented to my knowing? No matter what the Ashta-graha Kutam brings, it can only be a new phenomenon to be known by me. In knowing, where is the anxiety? My concern should be to economize thought as a prelude to elimination of thought. "Knowing" must cease so that "Knowledge" may prevail. How then can I waste thoughts on the future which is yet unmanifested effect in its own causal-condition? Whatever comes can only be another experience in the field of relative experiences. When it comes, it will be another ripple in a timeless continuity, raised by the preceding movement and raising the one to follow, an inevitable cascade of cause and consequence. To be an observer upon the shore is my privilege, and my freedom.

Then again to presume that the effect of an event upon the totality of the human mind can be known to this fragmented, individualized, limited intellect I have made of myself – which is the implication of a judgement being pronounced in the words "nothing happened" – is an obvious error. The event would have left its mark upon the predilections (vasanas) of the race, but with what effect in the womb of Time, is not within the province of my knowledge – the very enquiry would be wasted thought once more.

We shall not be concerned. We only need to know in the present who is that One in us who knows. To him whose mind is truly engaged in Self-enquiry (Atma Vichar), there is neither past nor future, and thus deprived of its moorings, Time sinks in the ocean of contemplation.

Let us realize that the Present is the product of the entire Past, and the Future is the Past modified in the Present. If an unintelligent Past with its hatreds, jealousies, passions and mutual distrusts has driven the world and the society into a sad plight of stress and strain, let our Present intelligence re-evaluate it, and right action modify it to the joyous life of Light and Bliss in this very same world.

Let this be then the subjective result of the devastating focus. When the eight "planets", which are the five instruments of perception, and Mind, Intellect and Ego join hands into a confluence, the mighty effects arrive. But whether the upheaval is to benefit us or to destroy us is to be decided by ourselves. To smother the lower tendencies with the effects of this "Inner confluence of the Eight" is the spiritual life; to yield to it the mastery that denies the higher, is materialism.

32
Prepare to Listen

Man seeks happiness in life. So does the moth that darts dizzily round the naked flame in closer and closer circles. Watch that moth ... Did it come here courting sorrow? Did it come in a spirit of sacrifice, however misguided? Did it come propelled uncontrollably towards known disaster? Not at all. That moth came here prompted by its sense perceptions, convinced that happiness consisted of flitting and dancing round the flame. It revelled in the memory of light and warmth, but the flame which gave them could give death too. This the moth failed to realise, and alas, was soon reduced to a charred heap.

Now watch the man who watched the moth. "Poor wretched moth" he says – but what of himself? He too is for ever in quest of happiness. This is well, for all life, at all times, is seeking a greater fulfillment, being persistently conscious of an incompleteness in itself. The tragedy is not at all that he seeks happiness, but that he pauses not a moment to analyse the means and the end, to assess awhile the outcome of all his past endeavors and the rationale of his present pursuits. He pities the moth. But the moth at least plunged towards one moment of ecstatic abandon, and made its first folly its funeral. Man, on the other hand, dances round the flame of desire his entire life, limbs burnt and bruised, flesh scorched, feet blistered, yet unable to stand apart, compelled by his cussedness to suffer and weep in his self-imposed ordeal.

Hinduism, the complete analysis of life, never asks man to give up happiness. It only asks him to give up the things that cannot possibly offer pure or lasting happiness, and search instead for the values that lead to abiding happiness. If a man is unhappy, worried, lacking in cheer, no matter how learned he is in our scriptures, know him to be a poor example of the ideal taught by our seers. For, progress in religion is progress in harmony. It contains in itself peace, quietitude, and beauty. It is a voyage into love, a vast love that encompasses all creation. Its emblem is a smile upon the lips; its strength, a gentleness of heart.

The child clings to the mother, supremely confident that its safety is thereby assured. The mother clutches the baby tight, afraid of all the tragedies that might befall, and hoping that none may descend. The father struggles for material prosperity, seeing security in the possession of things.

Time marches on. It brings health and wealth, and there is sunshine and laughter, and a frantic effort to forget that it cannot last for ever. Today all is well, but tomorrow will come. The day-after will come.

Now, when we are happy, let us examine happiness. When we are healthy is the time to build up the sinews further, not when we are in bed ravished by a burning fever. When we are crushed by tragedy, of which each mortal must meet his share, what power can remain in us to judge and understand?

Let us think on this. Can we gather happiness to ourselves and still remain unexposed to the ravages of unhappiness? It could be so if the two could be found separately. But in fact, closer than the rose and the thorn are they. What is happiness to the mind at one instant will itself become unhappiness as soon as the mind perceives a higher degree of the same satisfaction. This is true of all human experiences, for they are all relative, they exist as pairs of opposites, such as heat and cold, joy and sorrow, honour and dishonour, riches and poverty, life and death.

Then, he who would avoid unhappiness, must stop seeking happiness in the world outside. The world can offer nothing to man of which the worth, value or form time will not change, and with change, it will cease to be a source of happiness. This does not mean that he should possess nothing. It only means that he should develop a mental attitude of inner detachment from persons, places, and possessions so that he no longer depends on them for his completeness. What he has, or has not, would thereafter be of no consequence. Such a man always contributes more to the growth and glory of the world, for he strives not for his little self.

Hinduism does not attempt to define right and wrong in worldly acts, for no absolute concept is possible in the realm of relativity. There is no action so right that it cannot be bettered – and once bettered, from the level of that higher achievement, the earlier level must be declared to be wrong action. At each moment each individual acts according to the state of his knowledge then. In every action the conditioned personality of the individual is expressing itself truthfully, being true to its own total structuring. If there seem to be alternatives, the choice is already inherent in the priorities of the chooser. Thereby is action determined; through action comes experience; in experience is born new knowledge which endorses, alters or discards the old; and the new knowledge determines the nature of subsequent action. For ever there is the duality of knowledge and ignorance, without rigid determinism but ceaselessly in flux, and therefore causing changes in the individual personality which must however always and inexorably endure the limitation of its ignorance.

How then can actions limited by ignorance be "SINS" bringing upon oneself the wrath of a just God? Indeed He would be inviting the reasoned wrath of poor incapacitated mortals for adding insult to injury! "Sin" is not the right perspective, it is "ignorance" We are not sinners, we are ignorant ego-centres petitioning the world to give us what it does not even possess – abiding happiness – and reacting angrily, morbidly, violently, stupidly to the inevitable denial.

How true this is! How simple and beautiful and absolutely true this is! And he who knows this is soon on the path to love, tolerance, and peace. He condemns none, he realises that he is ignorant in one way and others are ignorant in different ways, but all are partly ignorant. Wherefore shall one man say to others, "My ignorance is all right but yours is bad"?

All that needs to be done is to eliminate this ignorance. What will remain is true happiness that is Bliss Eternal, incomparably greater than any fulfillment man has found till then.

How is this ignorance to be eliminated?

The Lord of Mercy[2] does not let His devotees call to Him in vain. When sincere hearts cry out to Him to lift the veil of ignorance, He sends a Guru[3] to them, sometimes inconspicuously, sometimes magnificently. Guru is Grace personified. He will show us the path of Self-Knowledge. Let our anguished hearts surrender to his

---

2 "The Lord" stands for the Absolute. The Reality, the Ultimate Truth – and is therefore the one and only Ultimate which all minds of all ages have signalled, regardless of social or religious affiliations.

3"Guru" is empirically the teacher of spiritual truth and the guide and aid to self-realization. However in its deeper import Guru is the inner potential to break through the veil of ignorance and to rediscover the Truth of oneself which is the Truth of God. So "He sends a Guru" need not mean that a god somewhere creates, instructs and deputes a noble human being – in its ultimate sense it means that the right attitude of the seeker invokes one's own inner potential to experience the Truth.

love. Let our tired minds yield effortlessly. Let the oft-deceived ego repose its faith in him. The words that drop from his lips rise from the Wells of Truth.

Hush... Silence now. Oh world of ceaseless motion, be still. Oh mind of endless agitations, please be quiet a while. The truth is about to be revealed. I must listen, listen, with my whole being...

33
On Happiness

Resist being lured and later fooled by happiness – that is the secret.

But too often we do not. Deluded, and thus made ignorant of a higher possibility, we cling to the tinsel that the sense perceptions gather for us from the varied woods of plurality. Like a mad man who, seated on a pile of stones, proclaims to the four winds, 'I am a Monarch, and this, my throne of precious gems', we hug a pile of material acquisitions and sense gratifications. Too lost in this empty worship of tin-gods, we have no eyes to see the irrepressible maiden Maya[4], standing at the door, playfully hiding behind her our Real Heritage, and smiling at our earnest preoccupation with passing fancies.

The thing that should put us on guard is not sorrow but happiness, not failure but success, not disappointment but fulfillment. Our real position is improved not when we borrow, but when we repay a debt. Yet hastily we consider ourselves gainers when we

4 That aspect of Shakti, the Creative Power, that causes the delusion of the unreal seeming to be real.

borrow and losers when we pay back. Same is the case with our experiences. *Happiness is the seed that germinates into the tree of sorrow.* Sorrow could well be the cause that carries in its core the blossoms of joy. It is within our power to turn grief to good purpose. Anchors are a burden not easy to bear for the ship that wants to press forward across the endless expanse of a sleeping sea, but the same steel weights are a source of strength and security to a ship that struggles for survival amidst the fury of foaming breakers and raging winds.

Let sorrows come. Bid them welcome, for they are the bitter fruits of our own misdeeds in the past. Cause must fulfil itself in effect, nothing can change that eternal law, so what matters now or later? Let them come and work their wrath and be exhausted. Why, or how, shall we deny the harvest of what we ourselves sowed? Now we are wiser, but there are waves from the past that must spend themselves upon the shores of future time.

Bid them come. The rust of past exposure to the damp and wailing winds of experience must be mercilessly removed before the burnished brilliance of the true metal can shine in its timeless glory. Let then the file be of rough texture, for faster will it wear the blemish away. The more cruel seems fate, know that a more benevolent deity is beckoning you.

But you cannot know this while you rise high upon every delight and crash below with every sadness. He who rides the waves must suffer all the anguish of the ocean's heaving breast, but he that stands upon the shore sees without being tossed about. So too must you stand upon the tranquil shores of knowledge, and watch with serenity the play of experiences.

This detachment must be cultivated constantly. The strength of mind for it, and the equipoise, can be developed by moderating a feeling of happiness that tends to fill one with every gain or success.

Remember, if you will not establish slavish contact with happiness, sorrow cannot establish contact with you. But seek one, and the other is there too.

The joys we wean out of life are ornaments of glass beads set in tinsel deposited in the vaults of time. The dim light of our befuddled minds startles the valueless trinkets into seeming brilliance, tempting us to gather them with both hands and hug them to our hearts. Alas, a scorpion sits upon each string, and the poisoned shaft is poised to strike!

34
On Limitation

The recognition is of the Divinity that is my True Nature. The expectation is that the True Nature will assert itself any moment. The wonderment is that even now, this very minute, I am not sublime, but remain human.

The recognition is not of the vasanas that hide my True Nature. The expectation is not that I, a bound limited entity, must wait upon Time, while the vasanas are exhausted, slowly or rapidly. The wonderment is not that I will, in some future moment, far off or not so far off, become sublime.

You are apt to retort: Am I not bound by my vasanas ? Do they not prevent me from rising instantaneously to God-hood ? You cannot say, "I am Brahman" and except a transformation. Face facts. Be realistic.

Alas, the accusation is in vain. Look deeper, what I am saying is this: Limitation is not in you. It is upon you. Let the limitation limit you, do not limit yourself. The law of the country says "You shall not take another's property". The limitation has been set on human behaviour. You have been subject to it all your life. Yet you have not been going about your daily life with the remembrance of this limitation. Nor have you been stealing as a consequence of your not remembering the law on the point. The limitation could not limit you, because, your true nature lay beyond the limits.

Even in the case of the thief who steals, is it not correct to say that he too does not, cannot, limit himself, but acts by his nature which is to steal, and is limited by the law when he is caught ? If he had limited himself, how could he steal ?

In this example, the thief may be caught, or may not be, for human law is not inescapable as it is administered by a human agency, but in Nature, which is the law of God functioning, the effect is inherent in the cause, and cannot be escaped. Apart from that, the comparison holds. Just as the thief does not and cannot limit himself, even though the limits imposed by law may limit his freedom, so too the Jeeva is, in its true Nature, Knowledge Absolute, and cannot bind itself by Avidya (vasanas), though Avidya may limit it.

To say that I know I am bound by vasanas is an intellectual contradiction. The Sun cannot know the meaning of Darkness. Can the Sun, hearing that the land was covered by darkness, rise over the horizon and see that darkness ? When I say I know it, I mean that I have knowledge of it, that the Knowing Principle in me recognizes it. Yet we say "I know I am bound by vasanas" meaning "I know ignorance". Is it possible ? "I see darkness", is it possible ?

What we think does not alter the relativity of knowledge and ignorance even within ourselves, but by thinking correctly about the relativity, subjective realisation is facilitated. By thinking "how can it be ?" we understand "It cannot be". We do not understand it, but understand that it cannot be. When that is understood, the realization comes "The other not existing at all, this alone is real". The sun heard from an outside agency that darkness existed.

The sun could only think in terms of light. "What form of light is darkness that I do not know it?". When the sun came to enquire, "what can it be?" the sun realized "whatever it was thought to be, it cannot be". It is the realization of Advaita, non-duality. The highest philosophy of Man has been called "non-duality", which means that duality does not exist. It is not the same as saying that oneness exists. Existence is relative to non-existence and in oneness there is neither existence nor non-existence.

Vasanas seem to bind us and we seem to be aware of the bondage. In the world of creation, relativity is the seeming Reality. But, there is a difference between the two attitudes with an expression of which this article began, and it is good to cultivate the right attitude. Indeed, it is no more a question of argument, it is a question of fact.

35
The Similarity

Because I understand what a rupee can buy, it is within my capability to recognise what a million rupees can buy. Knowing the nature of money through my experience of a small part of it, I can project my mind to visualise its highest potential. To a dog, a rupee means nothing, and consistently a million means nothing.

Anything created invariably implies that there must have been its creator with the requisite intelligence and the will to create. Therefore, it is natural for my mind, when it cognizes the mighty universe, to seek to comprehend what primordial urges in what ancient Awareness could have caused its emergence.

If the essential nature of the Creator differed from mine in magnitude, but agreed with mine in quality, I could aspire to contemplate His dimensions – otherwise, how would I ever know Him?

This is the great mercy then, that even now I am a tiny version of Him.

A sufficient, yet succinct, scriptural declaration has been that He is *Sat-Chit-Ananda*. Essentially He is Sat, that is, Existence in its entirety, or Absolute Existence. Not altogether unlike the fact of my own existence and of all else that exists, but not the same either. The existence I behold is ever within space, whereas space itself has to be contained within the creator, for the existence of space has to be precedent to the process of creation. I who am space-bound cannot dwell realistically on it, yet the concept shapes itself within the mind. If existence as variety is the world, and existence as individual personality is me, Existence Absolute as the source is not inconceivable. If I am capable of making this staggering extrapolation, it is because I too am existence; at least a fraction of it belongs to my personal experience. I know the currency!

In the familiar working of my mind, existence must mean at once the knowledge of existence. There has to be a faculty of knowing which encompasses a phenomenon to create a fact of existence. Therefore, my mind must be permitted to ask: If He is Sat (Existence), who confirms it in Knowledge?

Ah! says the scripture, the Existence that was stated is the Existence of Knowledge. Mind you (you mind!), not quite like what you are familiar with, which is *knowledge of existence*, but here it is *Existence of Knowledge*, or (to distinguish the Absolute from things Known and Knowable) Existence of Awareness (Chit).

My personal knowledge relates to Awareness as reflected light relates to the sun. Awareness is the pristine Totality that, remaining unaltered and undiminished, makes the mental modes of knowledge possible. Within my mind, I am a succession of flashes of momentary awareness of fragmentary existence, which are my thoughts. Thinking is the support of my living. "I think, therefore I am" is man ("cogito ergo sum" of Descartes). But awareness exists and of course needs no extraneous knower, so what can the Lord say in amplification of His Existence, of His "I Am" state, beyond indulgently (if somewhat abashedly!) yielding to our demand for an expanded description by telling us: "I Am that I Am" ("jehovah" of the Bible)?

Here again, I have the coinage and can transact. I can sketch His outlines in concepts of Absolute Existence-Absolute Knowledge (Sat-Chit) as I have personal experience of existence and knowledge.

I look at myself. True, I-exist-and-I-Know. But that is only the static fact of myself, that is not my dynamic story. For me life is a movement in the mind, thoughts weaving desires, senses demanding pleasures, limbs engaging in pursuits, a constant quest for happiness. To what purpose should Awareness exist?

The Vedantic Scripture says: Such Sat-Chit is itself Bliss (Ananda). You are a limited existence and therefore incomplete. Your desires reach out amongst the objects that populate the space that surrounds you, energized by your conviction that happiness lies in acquiring and expanding. Your knowledge is limited and is insecure in being circumscribed by ignorance. You are forever seeking abiding contentment upon the boundary where sky and space meet, while a life-time is lost in an unequal struggle. Total-Existence-Awareness has no gaps of incompleteness and therefore your concept of desire, nay, even motion, or time or space or causation cannot enter there at all. That state is naturally Bliss. It is allied to your feel of what happiness is, yet transcendentally so because it is not acquired or lost. Sat-Chit is itself Ananda, a restatement if you wish, but not a qualification.

Then, a speck of bliss resides indelibly in me too, does it not, seeing that I have knowledge of happiness?

One ray falls through the cavernous darkness wherein I reside, but it tells me of all sunlight, and of the resplendent sun. It stretches the whole way from me to the source, and for all its gossamer frailty, will serve as a ladder upon which the fairy feet of my mind may ascend into celestial climes.

And so, my Creator has not abandoned me. Though magnitude divides us, similarity provides a passage across the chasm. I am a spark from the conflagration. I am a drop from the mighty ocean. I am an atom from the cosmic dust. When I return to the fire, the sea, the universe, I shall know that my true nature never changed, that I ever remained an expression of Satchidananda.

36
Drawing The Line

Just the other day when Swamiji[5] was with us, sishyas (disciples) were narrating to him a discussion that took place a few days earlier when they had assembled along with some others. A defiant lady, who could not see any virtue in giving up meat-eating, had cornered them by asking them to justify their destruction of plant life for their food, and demanded to be told how if the one was to be condemned, the other could be commended. The sishyas wanted to know how Swamiji would answer the question.

We were standing around Swamiji under the open skies from which the sun was preparing to depart for the day. A cool breeze gently ruffled the grass which shook its mane in the mild sunlight. Calves and cows were ambling home, and the birds were bound towards their nests. All things wish to end their weary wanderings at Sandhya[6] time and nestle into the lap of abiding peace. And so does the mind too, in those still moments. So, we were happy to be in the serene presence of Swamiji then, and this is what he said:

---

5 *A revered Hindu spiritual master.*
6 *When day and night meet; dusk.*

I must eat, since I cannot survive without eating. The body is necessary for me to gain experiences, which give me knowledge, and so I must preserve the body. The material available in the world may be broadly classified as pertaining to the Mineral Kingdom (mud, stone, metal), the Plant Kingdom (leaves, vegetables, fruits), and the Animal Kingdom (fishes, birds, animals). A fourth and final category would be the Human Kingdom.

I find that I cannot eat matter of the mineral kingdom, I cannot gain sustenance from it, and still worse, it will destroy my body. Nature's laws do not permit it.

Not can I consider eating human flesh, for the idea is at once revolting to me, goes against my norms of life. It may sustain my body, but I cannot do it. I can't look at my neighbour's little child walking to my door and think: Ah, here comes my breakfast.

In other words, natural laws governing matter rule out my eating products of the mineral kingdom, and natural laws governing the mind rule out my eating human flesh. What remains are products of the plant kingdom and of the animal kingdom.

Now, I must in some measure disturb the peace, the harmony, the diverse existence of life since it has been decreed that eat I must. All that I can do is to choose that path which will result in the absolute minimum of disturbance. It is evident that life and experience are more vividly manifest in the animal kingdom than in the plant kingdom. Fear of death, desire for life, pain of destruction, are all more evident, appear to be more intense, in the animal kingdom. Therefore, I, who have to destroy something else to perpetuate myself in obedience to laws of nature that I cannot question or refute, choose to destroy the lesser than the larger.

Life must be taken to give life. Plant or animal must die to keep me alive. Then let it be the plant. That too I do in a spirit of meek surrender to what God has ordained, seeking forgiveness, and attempting to justify the sacrifice of life (of whatever order it be) by utilising it to develop a mind intent upon the Lord.

And so it is not a question of absolute right or wrong, but rather, one of drawing a line where it seems reasonable. I am standing at a station when I am approached by a hungry beggar. In my pocket I have a one hundred rupee note, a ten rupee note, a half rupee coin, and one paise. I feel straightaway that giving one paise would be totally inadequate, and giving the hundred rupee note totally beyond my means. I have to choose between the half-rupee coin and the ten rupee note. I decide – and most would endorse it – that giving the half-rupee would be the most appropriate course. Nevertheless it is conceivable that another in my place might give the ten-rupee note (and rue it at leisure!). It is all relative.

We listened and laughed and then we drifted to go our varied ways. Unnoticed the shadows had huddled closer and woven their black tresses together into the robes of Night.

Many an argument would be still-born if it were realized that no absolute conclusions are possible. All values are relative. Usage, or the law of averages, or the law of probabilities, gives them sanctity. These values are necessary for ethical living, for ordained society, for regulating mutual conduct. But for him who will travel beyond the shifting fantasy of relativity, Truth is not an opinion. It alone has Absolute existence or sanctity. It alone is un-questionable. The search of a hungry soul must take us beyond conduct, beyond all opposites – it must be for that transcendental Truth. Life will go on, societies will plod through time, changing, destroying, re-creating. Creeds will arise, survive, and perish. But you and I have a higher goal than abiding in time. WHO AM I ?

I am not the body. Not the temporal mind. I am Absolute, Timeless, changeless Consciousness.

AHAM BRAHMASMI, I am Brahman.

37
The Dance Of Shiva

To create a building, one must have the material with which to construct, and the plan according to which to construct. The human mind postulates that to create the universe the creative intelligence we call God had to have no less.

The "material" that God employed for creation was, if one may say so, VIBRATIONS. As walls are build with bricks, so with atoms molecules are built. But the atoms themselves are mostly empty space and, for the rest, infinitesimal entities in rapid internal motion. These entities, or charged particles, are only grossified energy, and can be converted into subtle energy as nuclear science has established. It was believed that all matter is built up of indivisible atoms, but now it is known that atoms are convertible into energy. Energy is force in motion. Motion moves matter in time and space. Matter, as we have seen, is energy. Seen thus, the subtle origin of matter is energy, and the subtle origin of energy is vibration. But vibration of what ? What is it that, vibrating, originated energy and devolved into matter ? It could not obviously be matter or energy, being the cause for both; so, in terms of our intellectual reasoning, it was "nothing". Then a NO THING vibrated and created the universe. NOTHING, of course, cannot have existence or properties or form. That Idea for which we have no words or expression, which is not a "Thing" and yet which cannot be understood through the word 'NOTHING', that is given the name "GOD". So when vibration was initiated in GOD, creation started. All that is seen in creation is only the result of this vibration.

The PLAN of creation is, expressed another way, the LOGIC in creation. The logic must be infallible.

Events do not always, or often, concern one individual. Many entities are involved. In marriage or death or birth, the mental or material conditions of a small group are affected. In an epidemic a community is affected. In war, nations are affected. A Napolean, a Buddha, A Christ, a Gandhi, or a Sage, leaves an impress upon the lives of generations then living and yet to come. The same event affects many in varied ways. The effect on each one must be suited to the logic of his personal existence at the moment, otherwise it would be an injustice.

Twenty people are killed in a train crash and thirty others are injured. Seventy others are not hurt, but are disturbed in different ways. The one single event of a train-crash must have been the logical culmination at that given moment in the lives of all those people, and yet different persons had to gain different experiences from the same event.

It could not be a case of concluding after the event that in a random way some had to die, some to get hurt, some to escape. There is no logic in that. There is only probability, without any other sanction than that of the law of averages. It cannot be that one or the other died, and that it was a matter of chance. That is against the observed behavior of Nature at work. Chance is the God of the atheist. No, what happened was the ONLY way it could happen. To say that after it happened would be sheer banality. Many people call this

Destiny. If that is what the word conveys, it is a word without meaning. It amounts to saying: "What has happened has happened". Where is rational sense in that ?

The reality is that an irresistible logic of causal sequence led to the event. Was there an awareness of it, before it happened, in any consciousness? Yes, there was. That awareness was ever there potentially in Knowledge Absolute, in the Supreme Consciousness, in the total cause which we can only know when it is manifested as effect. So then there must be a plan, unfailingly at work, a self-enforcing logic, that runs through all experience and all existence. How do those hundred-and-twenty persons happen to get aboard that one train, so as to share a common occurrence and be affected by it, each according to his deserving?

That is the law or the logic. It is the law given the name Karma. It is the logic of gravitation, first mental, then physical.

This is not the limited concept of gravitation described, explained and measured by physical science. The law of gravitation, in its truer import, is not merely that which governs the attracting force between bodies of mass; it is the law of attraction of the sense-organs to their respective sense-objects, of the experience to the environment, of crime to its punishment, and love to its reward – in short, of cause to effect. Therefore, the physicist's Law of gravity is but a fragment of the philosopher's Law of causality or Karma. The same conclusion is arrived at by observing that energy and matter are but two aspects of the same, and not unrelated to each other, and so if mass is subject to gravitation, the same law must function in energy relationships also and must have its place in the ultimate conclusion of vibrations in "Nothingness".

Science, if it has not already come to this understanding, is surely on the threshold thereof. But science can only probe nature as manifested effect, unravel it, understand it. It cannot go beyond observed facts and gain an indication of the Fourth Plane of Consciousness beyond sleep, dream and waking. The scientist who has studied all objects in the field of his perception must therefore turn his mind inwards for subjective enquiry. Anyhow the real scientist, who has understood the laws of Nature, is close to understanding the logic of Nature. Beyond that, there is nothing else to understand. Understanding must transcend into Experience.

Every great scientist stands at the doorway to the Temple of Ultimate Reality. He may not know it himself. The language of Religion may be alien to him and he may quarrel with anyone who calls him a religious person; but facts are not affected by what anyone thinks of them, but remain as the facts that they are. He is nearer God than many a professed devotee who is bound by vain actions. The key to the knowledge of the Creator is knowledge of creation. The key to the knowledge of creation is not to look for diversity, but for the Unity in diversity. The microscope and the telescope will reveal the physical content of creation, but for the INTENT behind creation, the mind must turn inwards to the source of Consciousness. Vibration here is the Dance of Shiva, the rising of a wave in the ocean of space. This is what has been superbly immortalized in the famous sculpture of NATARAJA.

38
Divine Mercy

Do not be so unkind to God as to ask in earnest "Why is God so unkind to me?" Ask instead, "Why has God's mercy towards me taken this particular form?" The mind has postulated, in its own terms aided by reason and abetted by instinct, a source of creation, a repository of all power, an embodiment of all virtue, a manifestation of pure love – and called that God. We must remain true to our definitions. Then, how can un- kindness come from the All-Merciful? Can cold come out of fire, or heat from the moon? Love alone permeates the cosmos.

There is no motive in creation, such as would, in human workings, tally purpose and action, cause and effect. But our mind rejects such a possibility and demands a postulate of personal intention. To accommodate the protest for a while the scriptures say "He created the worlds for His Leela", that is, to express and sport with the ebullient grandeur and joy and playfulness of His ever-peaceful and contented Nature. What Leela would it be if He had designed and built His dreamhouse out of bricks of sorrow and joined them with the mortar of despair?

No, that is against the very fibre of His nature which is Sat-Chit-Ananda[7]. In Ananda where is room for the piercing cry of agony?

This, then, was the great mercy. In creation insentient matter was bound by inexorable laws but sentient mind was an amalgam of freedom and bondage, freedom being the substance and bondage a mere shadow. Man had to discover the playful trickery, call the bluff and join in the laughter. The great game that God chose to play for His amusement was this: You think, so you exist. As you think so you become. Discover the origin of thought, the game is over, the freedom is total. Then He sat back, and watched man entangle himself in absurdities so vast and varied that He now shook with mirth, now frowned in displeasure, but remained apart, an uninterfering witness, for it was all a game, a delightful, ludicrous, amusing game in which the prisoner all along had the prison key in his own pocket. And this goes on!

Deception, nothing but playful deception. A movement from blind-folding to discovery. At times it seems to be regression, but really it is only progress. Like a fast- moving body slowing down: in terms of motion, there is unceasing advancement in the desired direction, but in terms of acceleration there is regression. So too, this Mind-Intellect, this conditioned self, this player in the hoodwinking game of Maya,[8] this amusing target of Leela[9] is ever moving forward nearer and nearer to the moment of liberation, the moment when the game is seen through, and it only remains to laugh and laugh – but it may appear as though one is sometimes moving backward, away from journey's end. In reality, it is the rate of progress, and not the direction, that changes. All experience is positive, so all existence is an assertion, and cannot be a negation even for a brief instant. The greatest tragedy, the bitterest grief, the most sordid mistake, constitute movements of low positive value, but are nevertheless

7 Existeyrce – Knowledge-Bliss.
8 The impossible becoming seemingly possible.
9 Exuberant mocking playfulness.

forward steps on the pilgrimage of life, for a negative excluded is also a gain.

That is the mercy. And this too, that not He, but I, am ever and absolutely the cause of all that befalls me. There is no cause unrelated to my own thought-processes – if there were, that would be tyranny, and could there be tyranny in the All-Merciful?

My miseries are not imposed upon me, there is no inevitability about them. Suffering is the price the mind pays for its lack of harmony with events. Seeing life as it unfolds itself, without fear or demand, and without the intrusion of memory, is seeing that cosmic love in action.

So first let me know life to be a game, to be played with assumed earnestness but without involvement, a make- believe, a merry mockery of self, which when done, shall but serve to raise resounding laughter of voices in unison, all His, or all Mine.

39
Whither Bound?

Shall I say "Happy New Year?"

And thereby commit a double error, the one of wishing the continuance of whatever the mind deemed to be happiness in its ignorant past, the other of surrendering to Time the right of assured and irresistible existence, making man subordinate to time?

Shall I think afresh, roused to alertness by the Grace of the Masters? If so I shall not walk in haste, lest I fall into the sudden pits of habit. I will pause – to think anew – to re-evaluate.

To accept a New-Year, to mark its beginning with my thought, and in doing so, to measure its duration with my mind, and thus to condition my existence with hopes and intentions – no, I refuse. If Time flows, let it not be because I permit it, but because I cannot *yet* stop it. With all my power I deny Time. If today I am a weakling whose defiance Time mocks derisively, it matters little to me. Once a bird set out to drain an ocean, and ultimately gained, in its own way, a victory of purpose over power.[10]

10 a mythological tale of ancient India.

I have bestirred myself with an awareness of my Real Nature. If there be limitations *upon me,* they are not part of me, they are other than me, they are no concern of mine. There are no limitations *in me,* I am free, I know my abode is within a silence whereto the clang of prison-chains cannot reach. And of all the chains, the last to leave him who gives himself up to their deceptive clasp will be the chain of Time. Time is the very metal that gives strength to all the fetters. When evil has been overcome and passion burnt by the fire of discrimination, greed and jealousy eliminated and anger quelled, the residual mind may yet last forever, caught unknowingly in the subtle nets of Time. Who shall free it then? Not time, for time will never end unless the mind revolts.

So I pray to you, dear Lord of Mercy, save me from the haunting persistence of Time, and give me the strength to live within the core of being where it cannot enter. For if I concede life to tomorrow, I proclaim death to yesterday; and this I cannot do. There are moments that must remain timeless to me... if they perish, I perish with them. Krishna lives and walks this earth: when love turns me into His beloved, the twilight hour will waft me His melody upon the breeze, calling me closer and closer. When I shed tears of protest that Mother has forsaken me, Sri Ramakrishna Paramahamsa will speak to me words of comfort and guidance... When I can no longer progress with the enquiry of "who am I?" Sri Ramana Maharshi will stir up a fresh ripple in the silent pool of the unknown. When I fall and lose courage, the Guru will, this instant, raise and lead me on. For They are HERE with me NOW, this must be so, or else, I am a rudderless boat on an angry sea. Yet I know I am guided by a Captain and secure from the tossing waves of time in my anchorage in the harbour of meditation.

There is no New Year then, nor was there the old. As for happiness, not only do I not wish for a repetition of sense-deluding experiences, but indeed I pray that I may be rescued from the memory thereof. Mother, forgive me for wandering into the woods, heedless of Your loving caution. The darkness has filled me with unnamed fears. I know You are near, Mother, but I cannot move towards You in the surrounding darkness. You, in Your grace, must reach out to me.

40
The Ultimate Salvation

ADVAITA means non-dual. In common understanding all experience is relative. Life's values are in terms of opposites, high or low, good or evil, pleasant or painful. The knower (subject) and the known (object) are forever apart. Then it must be so with the Creator and the created. But that raises questions of origin, method, and purpose of creation. Advaita is the Transcendence of the Absolute over the relative. It is the ultimate synthesis that eliminates linear dimension and establishes a seamless unity, an Absolute, unfettered by relativity.

Mind is always an amalgam of three inherent and distinguishable aspects: Sattwa standing for purity, love, nobility; Rajas for dynamism, valour, conquest; Tamas for indolence, greed, sloth and vulgarity. Varied proportions in the admixture express as the varied minds of a million beings.

Rising above Tamas, progressing through Rajas, and

> *finally leaving even Sattwa behind, man attains his salvation in the transcendental totally of Absolute Awareness that Advaita denotes.*

The arc does not know the circle; the circle cannot be ignorant of the arc. The part cannot know the whole; the whole need not even attempt to know the part.

Ethics is the arc.

At the same time, the arc contains in itself the sequential ogic whose extended rationale will make of it a circle. The recognition of its incompleteness is the prime demand that will start the movement towards completion.

Advaita is the circle.

Most philosophic creeds are segments, no doubt varying from a tiny arc to near completion of the circle, but definitely with two unjoined ends. Their content is effortlessly held in the fullness of Advaita, but they cannot discern their own limitations. To discern that would be to grow, and when an arc grows naturally, it can become nothing other than the circle.

The circle does not argue with the arc. Serene in the awareness of a completion that, returning the errant to the source, merges beginning and end into a beginning-less and endless unity, wherein very point has the same relationship to all the rest with the logical sequence never broken or varied, the circle whose perfection cannot be rendered more perfect, quietly smiles at the rantings and ravings of the deluded arc.

Truth is not a doctrine, for a doctrine however highly rationalised, is an opinion. Truth cannot be a way of life, for all ways of life are attitudes of mind, and mind whose other name is change cannot be the sheet-anchor of changeless Truth. Truth must lie beyond purpose, beyond method.

Evil and selfishness must be overcome so that the heart may expand in love and begin to shake itself free of its shackles – this every religion enjoins upon humanity. This is ethics. Then, the most ethical way of life should itself be perfection, and therefore, the ultimate Truth. Yet, these religions themselves have sanctioned varying and divergent codes of conduct, and what is ethical by one standard is unethical by another. For example, witness the habits of food or systems of matrimony acceptable to different climes and times.

Nevertheless, men have so enmeshed themselves in evil and selfishness that any message of love that can reach them and plant their feet upon a path of service has to b commended. The circle must rejoice to see the arc, with which it has kinship.

When the mind has reached the frontiers of ethics, it will learn to ask whether evil and selfishness alone are to be eliminated or whether attitudes of good and selflessness also are to be overcome. The question will arise whether life's purpose is living, be it by the noblest standards, and whether even living well for ever, having regard to time's unending tyranny, is not an ordeal too staggering to contemplate. The answers will provide the missing part that will make the arc grow into the circle.

This ultimate achievement of the mind cannot but be through the subtlest movement in thought. It is therefore understandable that its implications have given abundant scope not only for confusion, but for assertions of dangerous misapprehensions. Lesser mountains may have but hurt their climbers and then been conquered, whereas the loftier peaks have plunged into fatal fall many a valiant soul that aspired for the highest, but slipped. Because of it, will Mount Everest come down to the level of other summits? Truth remains calmly unconcerned. Those that will scale the tallest, risk the farthest fall. It is logical; it is right.

And so a generation of fallen men attributes its fall to the evil attitude of the peak, unwilling to face the fact of its own unpreparedness or unworthiness. Modern intellectuals of our own country assert that the concepts of our highest philosophy are responsible for the degradation of our nationhood; for the lethargy of our people today; and for lack of character (whatever that expansive accusation might mean). What wonder then that men of other creeds say the same things about us?

Religions which contained themselves within the ambit of ethical conduct had the limited objective of moving the human soul from Tamas to Rajas, from lust, greed, and apathy to restraint, generosity and universal concern. The concept was plain enough to appreciate, and when coupled with a promise of divine reward for good and a threat of punishment for evil, was capable of enforcing a movement of minds. An individual is a summation of the known and the unknown. The unknown is by far the larger arena, and is presided over by fear. So fear is a potent instrument to control the mind of man. Religions exploited this common weakness to enhance their reach.

A few amongst those thus propelled forward felt within themselves a fulfillment in loving without reference to reward or punishment, and they became the beacon lights of the movement, for the beauty and power of their gentle natures could not be doubted or denied. The vast majority however advanced in lesser or larger degree pushed by fear of immobility rather than by desire for the goal. The reason does not alter the result. There was movement. This is basically what happened in the West. The Western creeds seemed – but only seemed – to be superior to the Eastern.

Advaita alone transcended ethics. Conduct was not its criterion.

It saw that both Tamas (dullness) and Rajas (dynamism) are but degrees of imperfection, and even Sattwa (purity) is perfection only by comparison within the frame of relativity. It pointed out the transcendental plane of Pure Awareness as the Supreme Goal. Thus Tamas and Sattwa became the beginning and end of the circle, and Rajas the diametric opposite. Rajas could be distinguished easily by its movement, but subtlety was necessary to distinguish between total Tamas and pure Sattwa which became juxtaposed. The symptoms were seemingly identical – inertness, unconcern, self-centredness – but the entire gamut of creation and evolution lay stretched in the invisible chasm between the two.

And yet things went wrong even in the land that discovered this deep secret, when over the centuries the power of the revealed truth began to corrupt the very priests and preachers that held it in trust for humanity.

The glorious revelation of humble egolessness itself became the proud possession of the ego-centred. The knowledge of the science of renunciation was unchastely used for aggrandizement. What a mockery! What a fascinating twist in the history of Mind's emancipation!

So the land of Advaita has had to spend a part of her destiny bogged in Tamas, looking enviously and admiringly at countries that have attained to Rajas, itself momentarily ignorant of the potential for Sattwa clutched in the hand. Unlimited devotion to a limited ideal has apparently triumphed over the achievements of limited devotion to an unlimited ideal. But closer scrutiny must reveal that the longest list of the largest numerals cannot add up to infinity. Can perfection be envious of imperfection, or doubt itself?

Let it be. When it is known that Rajas cannot save, and the human soul despairs of its second stagnation, then the world must harken to Bharat (that is India) and her message of Advaita. Till then our

Motherland will wait, smiling and loving, not for Hindus alone, but for humanity; for she is the Mother of all, knowing no distinctions and all the beings of this earth are Her own children.

41
The Rightful Custodian

Gravity was not invented by the early scientist – it was identified. It was not a postulate, not a creation. It was a discovery of what was and had always been.

So too, the content of Hinduism was not the new product of an inventive or imaginative mind. It was the identification of the Truth of Existence. That truth had never been, and could never be, anything else, for truth can only be that which is ever-lasting. Truth cannot be falsified by time. Being the subjective Truth of oneself, that is to say, the centre of consciousness that confirms and validates existence, it had to become more than objective knowledge, it had to get transformed into subjective and transcendental experience.

The sages in cosmic memory are those who have thus realised this Truth and they have spoken of it through the scriptures. This as preserved in Bharath Mata is Hinduism. The philosophy of the Hindus is not a dogma or a creed, it is not an imposition or a command, it is an explanation and an invitation to every one to verify or deny those declarations of the sages, in personal subjective terms. It talks not of an age or a people, for fundamental Truth does not call for periodic restatement on account of changes and adjustments in social order. It concerns itself solely and directly with the meaning of life and the methodology of life's manifestation, and beckons all to the mastery one should acquire over the processes of time and place. That is philosophy. Now, what is religion?

The religion of a people is always the working-plan whereby the central philosophic concept is applied to daily living, so that the individuals may be guided knowingly, and even unknowingly, to walk the path that will take them forward towards the goal of ultimate fulfillment. Hinduism which clearly knew that Unitary Consciousness alone manifested as the universe of names and forms, and that he who perceived other beings and things was really undifferentiated from them all, gave mankind a whole system of rituals and prayers and sacred utterances designed and deviced to keep the individual on that path of progress, and transport him to his destination. The voyage is from individuality to totality, from the limited to the unlimited. The sages constructed vehicles which could be operated by the energies of life to serve the needs of mankind.

Beautiful cars too can kill the occupants when driven negligently. Mighty ships that can cross the oceans can sink through faulty navigation. The failure is not of the vehicle. So, if in our age the practices of our religion show flaws, these are flaws that misunderstanding and wrong usage and creeping errors have brought upon the basic structure. But the might and glory of Hinduism cannot be, and has not been, destroyed because of it. All that is needed is a little correction, a return to right application. One does not throw away the baby with the wash-water.

In spite of minor abberations wrought by the passage of time, Hinduism does not divide mankind into believers and non-believers on the guidelines of its own dogmas, nor does it reserve the meadows of heaven for its own tribe. To the one who accepts that all manifestation is only the one Divine in many forms with many names, how can there be anything alien? When any remembrance of the One Truth is worship, can one object to any expression of such remembrance? This is not just tolerance, it is not a suppressed resentment. It is a spontaneous indentity, it is a joy shared in the aspiration for a common goal.

Such is the Hindu's approach to the religions of the world, Muslim or Christian, Hebrew or Buddhist. When a Hindu sees a man at prayer, he too will by instinct fold his hands in reciprocity of an aspiring soul.

If this is not SECULARISM, what is?

Or else, that word has been mouthed and mauled by those who use words for common-place transactions in their casual lives, and have never felt the need to let the words take wing and reveal to the mind that joins in the flight, the real heights of their significances. If secularism means that the basis of morality and social justice should be non-religious, let the word perish – for mankind itself will perish, denied religion. It should be understood that religion is the method of living along the chartered course to self-realization. If by secularism is meant universal love of the Unitary Truth, the recognition of the Divine in all manifestations, then SECULARISM and HINDUISM are not two different words, they are synonyms.

So a Hindu India is itself a secular India. A Hindu India loves the worshiper at worship, and asks not his name. Nor asks "What God are you reaching to?", for the question is folly, there are not many Gods that have lost their focus in the Unitary Truth. All are brothers in the one undivided family of Truth, and he, my brother, can indulge the myriad musings of his mind to shape his own aspiration and all of them will be equally beautiful. And ultimately the God he seeks, and the God I seek, will not be the temporal forms of history, or the sound symbols of varied habits, but the Inner Reality of Oneself, that which pulsates soundlessly and timelessly in the Being as I-AM.

Hindu India will not interfere with any form of worship, for there is no need. It will not seek to alter others' ways, for all ways are symbolic and all symbols are but pointers. Hindu India knows that the only conversion is of the mistaken individualized ego-sense to a recognition of its Totality. Render divine what is now human – that alone is conversion.

May the leaders of our country begin to see this. Love cannot be taught to those that cannot feel an identity with the rest. But their hatred and intolerance cannot be given equal freedom in the life of the nation. They can be cared for and protected from hurting themselves and hurting others only by the love of those that cannot hate.

Hindu India cannot hate. If it did it would not be Hindu.

We are talking of love, not of timidity. Love is fearless. This too must be understood.

Are they listening?

42
The Deception of Time

"Beyond time and space" is often stated with reference to the Reality (or call it God). Is it a meaningful phrase? Can the mind sanction it? If the words can have validity, then time (or space) cannot be accepted in the common terms of our experiences. There has been an error some-where. Accept time, and there can be no Being, only a becoming, Deny time, and there can be no becoming, only Being. Time upholds creation, but does time itself have a leg to stand upon?

Our confusions when we strive to comprehend spiritual truths do not arise because the essential teaching is so *difficult*, but only because it is so *different* from the accustomed path.

Time is an impostor that has usurped the seal of authority, and merrily lays its false stamp of sanction on memory. Therefore, to our unsuspecting minds, Time has become the measure of Truth, and whatever has survived longer, has seemed, in some synthetic conclusion, to be the truer.

If it were indeed thus, Time alone should be the benevolent benefactor and the dispenser of all blessings. The ultimate rewards for our endeavours must even now be lying in the cupped hands of Time, to be given to us at some near, or far, moment of fulfillment. Otherwise we will be laying our hopes upon an altar of impotence and will be deceived.

Therefore, let us take a deliberate look at our urges and our motives, setting apart in ourselves the chosen from the choiceless, the ephemeral from the eternal, the beads from the string. And then we shall see in ourselves – in all of us so varied in views and wants and wonderment – yet a common core of mechanism and method that does not vary and cannot be denied.

To all of us, existence is synonymous with awareness, and awareness is a continuous relating of the individual with objects that are cognized, or memories that are recognized. A thing is newly seen, a word is newly heard, a taste is newly sensed; and it is interpreted in terms of prior knowledge, to become a new number freshly formed but of familiar numerals. Or a thing, a word, a taste, is recollected out of storage in memory and comes vividly alive in awareness. The objects of awareness change, but the expression of awareness never ceases, even deep sleep only tentatively halting the movement, not ending it. Whatever freedom one may claim to oneself in the use of the faculty of awareness, its ceaseless expression is a choiceless compulsion.

What reward can Time give us for this relentless toil and ageless submission? So long have we striven, but are as lost as ever in the wilderness of a myriad uncertainties. We can function till eternity in the pursuit of objective knowledge, sustained by memories that fashion our hopes, but we must remain on the brim of a mighty void from which the derisive laughter of Time will rise to haunt us.

This futile compulsion to remain a knower is twin to a compulsion to be happy. The whole movement of life-energy is to lead the individual from an accepted state of inadequacy and incompleteness, by an instinctive urge that demands fullness, into a different condition of such promise. Thus, driven by an inherent clamour to satiate desire as forged by memory, and thus earn repose in freedom from want, the exercise in futility is perpetuated.

For, what reward in changeless happiness can Time give us, itself being a succession of change, a creature of inconsistency? So far have we run, but the receding horizons will not come a step nearer. We may explore the infinity of space for a haven of enduring Bliss, but we must abandon our pursuit in the dungeons of nescience.

Another day, another place – and to trust that Time and Space will be our benefactors! We are not verbally conscious of our child-like credulity, but the accustomed current of our minds flows meekly down this ravine.

Divided into forms by space, and relegated to memories by time, we deem ourselves to be independent entities, and relate one to the other; we deem objects to be the dispensers of happiness, and reach out to possess. We accept without question that time has shaped our lives, and therefore concede without thinking that time is essential to reshape them.

If only we would depart totally from this easy slavery to a pretentious authority, and re-examine the facts of our being and our becoming! If only we would begin to be deeply concerned, each in himself, about "WHO AM I?"![11]

It takes an act of determined reassessment to see the truth, an act of Awakening.

---

11 Read Ramana Maharshi's "WHO AM I?" and "SELF-ENQLIIRY" (published by Sri Ramanashramam, Tiruvannamalai (T.N), India 606603).

43
Let Love Light The Way

Spiritual progress has to be funded from a deficit budget because it must uphold a pledge to produce more than is consumed and to give more than is taken. Its essence is to surrender, not to covet; its life-breath is detachment, not attachment-till lo and behold, in the hidden beauty of the mischievous circle that bends the acquisitive mind back upon itself to unite the farthest end with its earliest beginning, the perfect pauper discovers he is the only prince!

The conscience of the Hindus in the very land of their origin is stirring again after an era of neglect and indifference. The lapse is not beyond probability or pardon in the long history of a people that had scaled the peaks of perfection when civilizations elsewhere were stumbling in the foot-hills, but mere pride in the past is not solace enough. We have had our princes of compassion, and even more we have had our Sages and Seers who were manifestations of perfection bequeathing to posterity the identity of the Divine in the human. The teaching abides and awaits again the penitent listener. At this moment we stand upon the threshold, gazing out impatiently, poised for action, somewhat eager to march, but not quite knowing which road to take.

Here, then, let us pause a moment for there is the necessity to remember this – it is not the world that needs me, but I that need the world. Much before I can bring perfection into the world, the world can give perfection to me. I am too puny to stand apart and challenge the total will of cosmic creation, but by the right attitude I can *gain identity* with the whole, and *make that will my own.*

The right attitude is LOVE. As I stand here let me fill my heart with love. Christ saved but one leper; the welfare organizations have no doubt saved thousands. But that one saving will stir men's hearts down the corridors of history to eternity, whereas the thousands will be forgotten. That one saving was an act of spontaneous love of such natural perfection that Time wept and swore to remember forever. So let it be with our hearts. When we behold a leper at close quarters, let the kerchief come out to wipe a tear, not to shield the nose.

For, this must be humbly conceded – it will be easier to squeeze out a million rupees from the country to build a hospital than to squeeze out one tear from our own hearts for a suffering stranger.

When this love is with us, we shall add a new dimension to present-day concepts of social service – that man shall serve man not in charity, but in shame that all this while he deemed himself a thing apart.

How to gain this love? How to fill this dry and parched shell with the milk of kindness? By striving for knowledge and praying for Grace – how else? So let us come to feel more and more within us how all this is one, by applying the test of words heard, to our personal experience by contemplating the real or unreal nature of our pleasures and possessions, and by meditating upon *Sat, Chit* and *Ananda*[12].Such Sadhana (spiritual practice and discipline) will lead us to the goal.

12 Existence, Knowledge, Bliss – the three aspects of the Ultimate Reality.

Love must remain the substratum upon which activity is super – imposed. The world will reward us with an awareness of the effulgent Self if we humbly go to it with selfless love.

44
Happy Birthday to The Unborn

The same tale may be told another way:

When creation started, there was this enormous spherical cake, on which was playfully positioned a candle to celebrate the event. The ego, whose indulgence and amusement was the benign purpose of the creative urge, rushed upon the scene in faulty exuberance, its vision dimmed by the veil of ignorance, and indiscreetly seized upon the candle and not the cake, and started chewing upon it!

Essentially it is still doing that!

A candle is made of wax, and wax can be chewed on and on and on without being consumed (as any kid that knows its chewing-gum will confirm).

The candle is Time. The cake is the Universe of phenomena, wherein the ego-sense, if established in its true nature and freedom, could play and frolic amongst endless variations of charm and delight. But the ego becomes a victim of its unwarranted self-forgetfulness and perpetuates the error. It neither disregards time, nor swallows it – it keeps chewing upon it, seemingly anticipating an end to it, which of course never arrives. This unending process is the working of memory. *Time chewed upon by ego is memory.* Memory is the chewing-gum of the Creator! Any event in creation has no linear time in it, even as a dot has no area. It has only an immediate existence. But the ego wants to re-cycle experience, clinging to it by mistakenly deeming it to be the bestower of happiness, and therefore creates for itself a safe-vault, a treasure-trove, which is memory. Thereafter, the machine runs the man, and the ego's freedom stands subjugated to the dominance of memory, which perversely pretends to satiate hunger by secretion of saliva through the glands of desire. The ego swallows its saliva but cannot obtain such sustenance from it as can give back to the ego the strength of its True Nature. The Absolute is not an offering of memory.

Such an ego-person am I, and if such a one you too be, my friend, we are looking at Bhagavan through the irrepressible mechanism of our habituated memory-systems. We do not and cannot have any other parameters for our empirical assertions. So, true to ourselves, we declare "Bhagavan[13] was born on 30th December 1879 and died on 14th April 1950". And with loving remembrance, we celebrate the anniversaries. Yet our minds have set him apart from ourselves as a manifested Perfection beyond our imperfections and therefore as Infinity beyond our finitude, as Eternity beyond our evanescence. So, lest we become tainted by sacrilege, we seek the reassurance of our loud voices protesting, "But our Bhagavan is with us even now. His Presence can be felt by us. Did He not Himself say, 'Where can I go'?"

Here a seemingly irreverent question can have pertinence and utility for us. My own grand-pa, about as good and bad a man as I am today, died a few decades back, and as wailing voices proclaimed, attained the Feet of the Lord (hoping that he would be able to identify them if he was shown them). Let me presume that a similar statement

13 The reference is to Bhagavan Ramana Maharshi, The Sage of Arunachala.

could be made of your G-pa, (or G-g-pa) – no offence meant.

Now, it has been clearly and irrefutably perceived and declared that life-energy manifesting as consciousness expresses itself through a body which is only its vehicle, and what is seen as living and dying is only ego-sense inhabiting or vacating the body-vesture. As long as the fragmented ego-sense persists with its residual desires, so long will the individual exist centred in oneself within a felt body – subtle or gross being only relative terms in retrospect. So departed G-pas continue to have existence and experience, with that good old twinkle in the eyes reinforced in the new-found freedoms. But there is no spiritual transformation, much less elevation, in all this. Death is not a bestower of knowledge of the Self. Disembodied G-pas go about their ways in their subtle bodies seeking pleasure and hoping to avoid pain, even as they did amongst us in their gross bodies (and as we are doing now), desire-propelled individuals upon the turning wheel of rebirths, till eventually liberated by abidance in the Unitary Truth of oneself.

We have to distinguish between death of grand-pa and what seemed a similar 'death' of Ramana Bhagavan.

If death is separation of a partite consciousness from its total identity with a body, 'death' was an impossibility to him we called Ramana. For, there was no individuality that dwelt as "I, Ramana", cognizing "you, devotee" or "it, the hill". My body is suffused by an I-sense, both of them merging to perpetuate a self-imposed limitation through this ego's ignorance of its Real Infinitude. But Ramana is not the body-identified limited 'I'. Ramana is that Self-Aware Infinitude. In that isolated body that you and I perceive as Ramana there is no inhereing self-deluded ego-identity limiting itself to that body. In that Total Stillness, how can there be the movement into 'death' which to our perception is always an upheaval upon the current of time?

It follows that Ramana-form when 'alive' amidst us was even then a particle of Himself, a ray of light that beckoned the eye to discover the Sun at its source, a touch of love that led the mind into the ocean of compassion. As He was Perfection Itself, every response from Him had in it all the potential for our perfection; the fulfillment or failure of the benediction lay in our receptivity and capacity to benefit, not in a largesse denied. That our eyes saw His body and our ears heard His voice were aspects of grace poured into our cups that were already overflowing with His Grace – their denial now is not a deprivation.

Memory can and does resurrect its contents. It can bring to me now the image of the remembered G-pa, as it can the image of my Ramana Bhagavan. But in the interplay of recall and response, of longing and embrace, how can the voyage of a demanding soul into the unchartered expanse of Infinity be matched even remotely by associations locked in temporal and spatial sequences?

Ramana was or Ramana is? That is the question.

My grand-father was or is? That is the seemingly irreverent paradigm that focusses upon the core of the question, to validate the answer in depth.

As long as the question is in terms of temporal tenure, 'was' and 'is' would both be admissible for any and every person, 'was' referring to the manifested form and name of the destructible body, and 'is' referring to the energy that expressed through it. This energy would retain continuity, though losing specific identity, through changing form- associations. Such continuity of existence may be reason for solace to the grand-son left behind, even as it would have been a relief to the 'dead' elder when death revealed itself to him as only a changed status of life. But that is not the answer to our question born of a quest, an agonized reaching out for support and succour as we grope for redemption and desperately need the comfort and confidence which our loving Bhagavan amidst us in palpable terms would bestow upon us.

And it is there, and then, that Bhagavan says "I am with you. Where can I go?" Listen to the voice of Silence that uses words that are transmuted. "I am" is not for validation by the cognitive senses; "with you now" is not circumscribed by time; "with you here" is not encircled in space.

It is the call that, heeded, shall make the moment an eternity, make the microcosm an infinity, transform the relative I to Absolute Being.

As long as time is believed to be a linear stretch between past and future, linking memory and expectation, so long must consciousness continue to exist and experience. To think that death of a body is the death of the embodied consciousness is the simplistic lie that deludes the unthinking ego. But even the alerted ego can land itself in the second and subtler falsehood that transcendence of the bondage of time is attained by being coeval with time. That is only an ETERNITY OF TIME. Reality is TIMELESS ETERNITY, and that is the meaning of HERE and NOW.

This is what our Bhagavan has vouchsafed to us. He alone could, because LONG BEFORE TIME COULD WRITE RAMANA'S OBITUARY, RAMANA WROTE TIME's OBITUARY.

Part III

NARRATIVE

45
'I AM NOT THE DOER'
An Interview of the Author

This is not a writing by the author, *but an article about the author, based on an interview by Pradeep Krishnan for the well-known magazine* Life Positive *in its August 2018 issue.*

We are grateful to Life Positive *for their generous permission to reproduce the interview here.*

Sri Dwaraknath, in conversation with ***Pradeep Krishnan***, shares his views on Creation, Karma and God, influenced by the teachings of *Sri Ramana Maharshi.*

Sri V Dwaraknath Reddy, born in 1924, is a seeker, author, lover of nature, a humanist, and a poet. He is the former Chairman of the Nutrine Confectionery Company and, for decades, has been engaged in spreading the teachings of Sri Ramana Maharshi. After three decades at the helm of the company, he had relinquished the corporate reins and settled in the vicinity of Ramanasramam, the spot sanctified by the continued presence of Maharshi.

Author of a dozen books on spirituality, including The Dicey Problem of New Age Science; Birth, Play and Finale of Mind; The Physics of Karma; Death Was Never Born, Life Never Died. *Sri Reddy, a postgraduate in Chemical Engineering from the USA, is an original thinker and has the ability to lucidly explain complex ideas to the reader. In his writings, he blends rational precision with a deep understanding of philosophy, focused on the core teachings of Sri Ramana Maharshi. Commenting on them, late M.P. Pandit, savant of Sri Aurobindo Ashram, says, "It is the authenticity of his experience – psychological and spiritual – that touches the reader and makes him as humble as the writer himself."*

Last year, during my annual pilgrimage to Sri Ramanasramam in Tamil Nadu, I had a chance to browse through his book Can God Improve My Balance Sheet? *in the ashram library. "When you aspire to attain success like never before, your plan of action cannot be to conspire to make luck strike you and lightning strike your competitors! Though commendably simple and straightforward, the strategy is beyond your powers of manipulation. The success you desire must be won by invoking the inner potential in yourself. You must become the best you can be."*

The above passage prompted me to meet the author. My wife and I visited Dwaraknath Reddy at his residence, situated just across Sri Ramanasramam. He has been living there for the past 35 years with his adopted daughter Sandhya. At the height of success in business, he had handed over the family-owned company to the younger generation and set up the Ramanarpanam Trust, under the leadership of his daughter, Anita Reddy, to help the poor and needy. So far, the trust has donated nearly Rs.35 crores in charity, benefitting about 20,000 people and over 3,500 children. Mostly this donation is from his personal share of corporate earnings.

About his writings, he said, "I write for consolidating my contemplations, I write for self-education. This is my meditation."

To my question about what prompted him to settle near Ramanasramam, he said, "All that I have known and all that I seek to know is contained in the manifestation of Bhagavan Ramana Maharshi. So, I have come to reside where His bodily presence stayed almost a lifetime. His silent gaze dwells on me. Here is the focus that I must merge with."

Tell us about your family background and the setting up of the Nutrine Company...

Ours was an agricultural family from Chittoor district of Andhra Pradesh, with a good cultural and ethical background. My parents were pious and generous.

My father, late B.V. Reddy, had high values and ideals in life, thanks to his education, a B.A. from Theosophical College, Madanapalle, founded by Annie Besant. Later, attracted by the vision of late Jiddu Krishnamurti, his son Dwaraknath Reddy, became a member of the executive committee of the Rishi Valley School, along with notables like Sri Achyut Patwardhan, to which school B. V. Reddy sent his three sons, Surendranath, Raghunath and Dwaraknath.

After completing education at the Rishi Valley School in 1940, I did my B.Sc. Tech course. Thereafter, with an aim to set up a sugar factory in our district, my father sent me to study Chemical Engineering at the Louisiana State University, USA. Meanwhile, at a time when Parry Company had the monopoly, the Nutrine Confectionery Company commenced its operations in 1951 from Chittoor. On my return, I was put in charge of the company, along with my elder brother. In course of time, the Rs. 5 lakh company became the market leader with a turnover of Rs. 300 crores.

How did you develop an interest in spirituality? What was the turning point in your life?

As a student of science, I always had a rational and scientific mind and had no belief in God. But, when I was 35, the sudden death of my brother Surendranath (due to cerebral haemorrhage), who was very close to me, completely shattered me for several days. As there was no one else to manage the company, somehow or the other, I was pulling on. Soon, questions about life, death, and God, cropped up in my mind: If there is justice in a God, why did my brother die at such a young age? Then one day, someone suggested listening to the talks of Swami Chinmayananda. When I came to know that Swamiji is taking classes on Mandukya Upanishad in Madras (Chennai), taking three days off, I went there. At the venue, hearing the melodious *bhajans* sung by Swamiji's disciples, for no reason, tears started rolling down my eyes. I am sure it was not because of my brother's death.

For three days, Swami Chinmayananda expounded the concepts of mind and matter, work and worship, creature and creator, love and lust, and shadow and substance to the huge gathering. His words, "The truth of that God is the truth of you," explaining the concepts of *Aham Brahmasmi* and *Tatvamasi*, stirred something within me. I felt the teaching was amazing. He took absolutely contradictory aspects but logically equated them and proved that it was the absolute truth.

I listened to him with rapt attention and, slowly and steadily, the concepts of absolute and relative became clear to me. I understood that one functioning through consciousness is God, which is called Brahman or the totality of consciousness. That Brahman alone became many. Listening to Chinmayanandaji was the turning point in my life.

Then how did you develop an interest in Ramana Maharshi?

Chinmayanandaji was the one who put me on the track of spirituality. After listening to him, back in Nutrine, I started reading his books and contemplating on the ideas. Soon, he became my Gurudeva and the relationship grew to such an extent that I became one of the Trustees of Central Chinmaya Mission Trust, a position I held for about 15 years. In the meantime, I happened to read selected portions from Ramana Maharshi's *Who am I, Self Inquiry,* and *Talks* that generated great interest. I felt that it contained the essence of the scriptures: the Gita, the Upanishads, and the Vedas. It was Chinmaya, the great teacher, who brought me to the teachings of Bhagavan Sri Ramana, the Realized Master. Before long, though I have not seen Ramana in person, his words started penetrating deep within. I was convinced that Ramana, the ultimate Guru, helps one and all to realise the Vedantic truths of *Ayam Atma Brahma*, *Prajnanam Brahma*, and *Aham Brahmasmi.*

How do you view the manifestation of Ramana Maharshi?

A self-realised sage like Ramana Maharshi is a rare event of supreme splendour, manifested in the cosmic play. The world sees him as an exquisite manifestation, an exemplary person, a rare gift of time. Such a one lived amidst us, for a duration of time, and is recognised by a body-form. In terms of our relative reality, we say Ramana 'lived' and 'died'. History recorded that he was born in 1879 and attained *samadhi* in 1950. But Ramana Maharshi 'IS'.

"In the silent depths of the ocean flow
Mighty currents unseen
In the truth of this moment lie
All the ages that have been."

You had written a book on the law of karma. Please explain its workings.

If any society has to function in an orderly fashion, there must be some methodology, establishing the order that we call God or Creator or Nature. The cosmos is governed by the laws of gravity, magnetism, nuclear forces, etc. Similar is the role of karma in one's individual life. When the bulb that gives light suddenly gets fused, did the electricity die? It exists continuously. Likewise, when a conscious ego, a person, dies, the bundle of accumulated *vasanas* remains and gets carried over to another life, causing another birth. This continuity of cause and effect is called karma. Just as gravity is established by the intelligence of God or Nature, consciousness of a being works as karma. What remains unfulfilled at the time of death remains incomplete and results in taking birth again – that's how karma works.

Do you think the planets influence one's life? How do you view astrological predictions?

Creation is holistic and in the web of causal interconnected strands of action, everything is the cause and effect of anything. Sage Nisargadatta Maharaj declared, "The stars influence you and you influence the stars too." So, planetary influences are not the intimidating one-way traffic that mortgages one's future to astrology. It is probabilistic and not deterministic. The path, speed, directions, and destination of a ball placed on the ground and hit can be predicted with accuracy by applying the laws of physics. However, the path of a human being cannot be determined as he is bestowed with a consciousness and will. So let us leave our worrying to the planets and live our lives with will, effort, and self-confidence.

The understanding of the Universe is baffling. Why are we born?

The Masters tell us it is to find out for oneself the reason for one's birth. Understand that there is absolute reality and relative reality. The truth is 'life' never died and 'death' was never born. Like a dream, death is a falsehood. During a dream, though you are asleep, you are alive. Realise that "we are immortal through renewed mortality."[1]

What is the purpose of this Creation?

Science knows everything about the 'content' of Creation, but nothing about the 'intent' in Creation. 'Intent' does not mean the will or purpose of an inscrutable God, and God should not be taken as a locus outside Creation, shaping it arbitrarily. Intent means a law of consciousness that ensures a continuity of causal flow so that the end is a return to the beginning, all the movement is sequential, and nothing is random. Intent is the infallible rightness in the Law. If God is posited as the law-giver, he is the Law too. I say God would then be equally comfortable with such an understanding on our part, for we would have at least moved beyond insisting that 'chance' is the arbiter of cosmic harmony.

What according to you is the problem of New Age science?

"God does not play dice," said Einstein. In a note of dissent, Stephen Hawking said, "God is quite a gambler." These quotes discuss whether Newtonian determinism or quantum probability is the truth in Creation. But Truth or Reality cannot be extracted from relativity. It is Absolute. Therefore, it needs to be said, "God has no need to play dice, for He owns the casino." His right hand picks up what the left hand may lose.

In fact, Hawking was saying that the scientific concept of matter was shifting from the theory of relativity to quantum theory with its probability functions. He was convinced that chance (probability) remains the supreme arbiter of what was, is, and will be. With both supreme scientists, the word 'God' was a fleeting digression. Scientific investigation of reality progresses from speculation to experiment to observation. Ideas thus get rejected or accepted, and in the course of time, what was accepted earlier is abandoned

1 Quote: Sri Aurobindo

and new concepts hold sway. We, the conscious individuals, are playing the dice in the casino of objective knowledge, within the four walls of relativity. However, the Absolute includes and exceeds all of relativity. Infinite Absolute Reality has been given the word 'God'. The limited got the name 'Man'.

What is your concept of God?

Sat-Chit-Ananda, these three words give meaning to our personal existence, pursuit, and purpose. They denote the three primordial and compulsive aspects that energize life. The Sat aspect of Atman is what penetrates through the mask and instinctively gives man his indelible concept of eternal existence. The Chit aspect of Atman is what equates life with thought. The Ananda aspect of Atman beckons to the confused mortal through all the layers of gloom and he strives for lasting happiness. Ignorantly, man attempts completeness by material acquisition and is fooled. The fact of *Sat-Chit-Ananda* in each individual, in whatever state he may be, is the link that was never broken, the salvation that was never denied, the perfection that was never removed, and the light that was never extinguished. It is ever there, even now, not a thing to be gained hereafter. God is, even now, the Truth in man. How beautiful, how heartening, how divinely merciful.

"Some say acupuncture
is good for the body.
All saints say ego-puncture
is excellent for the mind."

How do we solve problems in life?

Really, what is a problem? Obviously, as long as one's desires are fulfilled, wants satisfied, and nothing is happening contrary to one's wishes, there is no problem. Is there? For one, the present situation becomes a problem because it is not taking shape the way one wanted it to. Understand that it is taking shape the only way it can, given the compulsion of the law of causal manifestation, given the precedent and prevailing forces that have produced the natural result. The fault is in one's faulty understanding of reality. It is only the mind of man that thinks that such an error has taken place. So I say, man 'has' no problem; man himself is the problem.

"Typhoid may sometimes
infect the body;
I-phoid is the constant disease
of the mind."

\What message would you like to give to the readers?

Understand 'who am I' and that the ego is not the doer. When doership goes, the ego-sense transfers itself to becoming a devotee. The purpose of doership is only to find out that one is not the doer. The highest achievement of the intellect is to learn that God is self-revealing. You do not require a torchlight to see the sun. Whatever is being done through the ego-sense is pervaded by *Brahman*.

This interview was published in the August 2018 issue of Life Positive magazine and has been reproduced here with the kind permission of its Editor.

46
Autumn Leaves

The author's father died on 27th, October 1964. This article was written then.

He lost his father a few days back.

Four years earlier, he had lost his elder brother. Healthy and strong at thirty-seven, smiling and cheerful, good and generous, with all the promise of the blossoming years yet unfulfilled, he was there at dawn but gone by noon.

That had posed many questions – of life and death, of love and loss, of the unfathomable finality of an irretrievable moment just past. And he, surviving in lonely sorrow, had dared to ask whether there may not be other measures of time and of fulfillment by applying which the conflicts of our common understanding would cease, and the sanction of a transcendental justice become acceptable.

Then had come to him the merciful Teacher, and too, there had awakened within him the capacity to love such a one.

That was four years ago. And now he was without his father. Death had visited the home again. No visit would be the last.

Sorrow is not a thing for denial. It belongs to the mind, as moonbeams belong to the moon. It is a thing to be witnessed. It is not without beauty. It has depths, oh what depths, and it surely has a purpose.

Does one lose a father, a brother, a child, a spouse? One only loses a relationship. No, not even that. One only loses the immediate form that lends reality to the relationship and cohesion to the concept.

So he wrote to the Teacher: "Our dear father, you are ever with us. We are one with you in love". And Gurudev[1] replied, "Blessed children, this is the way of life. The past departs on the shoulders of the present. The present must learn joyously to bear the burden. Devoutly loving the present, act on inspired to build the future. This has been the way of life – and when has it been otherwise? I am thrilled to note the devotion of the villagers towards such a lion amongst men. Your father never was a man of words and emotions, but he was throughout the man of action. He spoke with actions, and his achievements spoke for him. Keep up the tradition. May you have enough breadth of shoulders to carry all the burdens that come to you. With surrender and devotion unto HIM, act diligently. Obstacles will wither away."

The four years since Death's first visitation had not been in vain. This youth had striven to see the Law at work. He had grasped this from his study: Matter is not involved, for it has no mind: Mind is redeemed when it has no will; Will is redeemed when it has no ego; Ego is redeemed when it loses itself.

All that the good Lord has said of Himself is true with reference

1 Loving, reverential address to One's spiritual master. (This was in 1964. The quotation is from a letter written by Swami Chinmayananda)

to the core of each individual existence. "Na mae Parthaasthi Kartavyam"[2]... "There is nothing, oh Partha, that has to be done by Me". So all of us should say: There is nothing that HAS to be done by anyone. There is no preference, hence no anxiety, hence no bondage. All action is in Him who is the Purusha.

Not that he did not weep. He wept, and saw the weeping thereof.

Many came. Some came to wipe his tears. Some came to shed their own. Others came because that day there was grief in the air they breathed, and it is easier to grieve with others than to grieve alone – yes, so much easier. But of them all, the coming of one remained a refreshing memory when all had come and gone. That one was a kindred soul, who had been blessed at an early age with a longing for spiritual evolution, and had surrendered at the feet of a Divine Master. He sang in ecstasy, but was not his life itself an ecstatic song? He sighed at sorrow, but he would have sighed at happiness too.

Letters came in large numbers. "How kind people are," he thought, they feel another's sorrow and try to make it less." And of all the letters, the most heart – warming, the most strengthening, elevating, were those that he received from his brothers and sisters in the satsanghs[3] of his spiritual quest. Invisible strings of attachment were vibrating, making soft music, a gentle melody of simple love, not so much of one for the other, as of both for yet a Third, who when the triad was resolved remained the Only One. What was shared was love of God.

There were those that wrote "time is the only healer," but he, now grown a little wiser, sadly realised the negativity of such consolation; for it meant that forgetfulness is the final tribute to love. No, he would rise above that.

---

2 Bhagawad Gita, Ch.III – 22.
3 Gathering of fellow-devotees.

A few there were that spoke of the cruelty of God, and this it was that hurt him. How can men call Him cruel who is Pure Love? He himself had been blessed beyond reason, had been granted a wonderful father for so long, had known the full giving of tender hearts, had been placed at the lotus feet of Gurudev and allowed ample opportunities to serve, to strive, to prosper, to ponder, to learn, to grow. Oh beloved Lord, Thy will be done.

47
A Visit to Uttarkasi

(About a hundred miles beyond Rishikesh, several thousand feet above the Gangetic plains, on the banks of Bhageerathi, is the small town of Uttarkasi, till not long ago a serene halting place for persistent feet pacing the winding path to the higher reaches of the Himalayas, and, too, a haven for many a seeker after spiritual fulfillment; though today its strategic importance on the nation's frontier, for defence or destruction in a world divided against itself, might have distorted its face and scarred its soul.

Upon a rocky slope here, somewhat removed from the habitations, overlooking the river and surrounded by mountains that rise abruptly, in a little Kutira (hermitage) had lived that spiritual giant Tapovan Maharaj, whom other masters acclaimed as a Teacher-of-teachers.

In 1963, the author had the good fortune to be in a small

group that went there with Swami Chimnayananda, the renowned disciple of the Master. This article was written in those sacred precincts then.)

"Mother, I listen for thy song, but I cannot hear it. I cannot hear it, Mother, for your song is Silence. But when I try to catch your melody in my heart, I hear the vibrant Sruti of the strings you pluck, and for granting me this at least, I love you.

I hear the eternal elemental chorus of wind, water, and wild mountains. It speaks to me of your mighty power, your terrible wrath, your irresistible strength. When I tremble and seek your protection, it speaks to me of your immense kindness, your abiding love, your tenderness.

Let me linger here awhile, Mother. This bruised mind must hearken back to the beginning of memory when you held me in your lap.

Here in this valley Tapovan Maharaj had made his abode. Come along the foot-path, go through the little gate to the left, climb a short flight of stone steps, and you are at the Ashram. A little room, and a small verandah in front, that is all. So tiny? Not really, for it was vast enough to contain for over thirty years the sweep of his intellect and the immensity of his love. Here came the young seekers, thirsting for those magic waters of knowledge that bubble out of the fountains of Subjective Experience and they emerged into the world of men, after months or years - or was it a millennium? - to give of their love and learning.

In this verandah they sat, looking across the narrow valley. The ceaseless roar of Bhageerathi below reached them as the bluish-green waters broke into white foam upon the rocky bed and hastened beyond the curve. They could see the steep slopes of the hills rise from the river bank to the towering cliffs on top.

> *Stand apart, oh Intellect, and watch this scene. Be the Ashram, under whose sheltering roof the Ego may sit and witness the world beyond. From here, it is a small world – just the river and the rising hill. See how the waters come and go, the bank makes no efiort to hold on to them. Let your thoughts flow on, too, while you watch them without involvement. Wherefore shall you hasten one thought in revulsion or cling to another in attachment? Vain is that attempt, the effort is wasted, failure is the only fruit.*

Here came men of all types and attainments, to gain from Tapovanji such blessings as they could or would. The great Master knew each one's limitations and trends instinctively and gave to each what each could benefit by. To the men of unreasoned faith, he spoke exultantly of the might and power of various places of pilgrimage and exhorted them to visit those Shrines regularly. To the newly-arrived, sincere but untried Brahmachari, he made austerity the cardinal principle of spiritual aspiration and enjoined him to live a life of mental discipline. To the elderly sanyasi of ripening years, he pointed out that "in the three periods of Time, as a limited individual I was not, am not, nor ever shall be; that being so, how can there be success or failure, joy or sorrow for me? I am Being, never bound by becomings". The Master thus guided a hundred minds along a hundred paths towards the One Goal, musing inwardly that all knowledge acquired by the mind is but another facet of ignorance, for speech belongs to the realm of the false, and Silence to Truth.

> *You cannot remain content ever, mind, you must ask what lies beyond this hill! Saving grace has limited the view to bring contentment nearer to you, yet you*

> *cross the boundaries in quest of anxieties. Well, since you ask, I will tell you the secret truth. Before you asked, not even "nothing" was beyond the hill, but when you asked, Space was born there. "And then?" you ask. Well. I will tell you this too. When you asked that, Time was born. Now keep quiet. I know you are rearing to ask "Why"? but I will not answer. We will not resurrect causation.*

Next to the Ashram is a small structure which serves as kitchen and contains a spare room. Here the subject of our narration, the aspiring Sanyasi, resided for some time. For the rest, he lived at various Kuteers. He sat at the feet of the Master for an hour or two a day listening as he taught the Upanishads, and then spent several long hours in discussions with other students and Swamis. Once when studying Mandukya Upanishad, he became emotionally and intellectually so overpowered by the highest concept of Advaita, by the unreality of the dream that is both mind and matter, that he felt a deep urge to go into the silent seclusion of Ekantavasa (voluntary solitary confinement). He had heard of a temple that lay behind a village which sat perched half-way up the slope of the hill beyond the river, a temple that was unfrequented, and there he decided to dwell all alone. So one morning, ere yet the dawn had brought the faintest glitter to the gliding waters, he set out on his journey with his books and a few belongings. He had walked a mile, negotiated a foot-bridge across the river, and was progressing along the farther bank, when it happened that Tapovanji seated himself in the verandah of the Ashram and gazed meditatively across the valley. Suddenly his eagle eyes discerned even in the early light a familiar figure marching with purposeful tread, and receding up the slope. Soon he had understood the situation and hastened a man after his errant disciple. When a crest-fallen and rather confused youth returned to the feet of the Master, he was told "Stay here in the company of other Mahatmas. Alone in the village there are temptations and who will help you there? You are not yet ready for Ekantavasa; stay in the company of the good and train yourself for another three years". This episode impresses upon aspirants the true significance of detachment. It must follow in the wake of right knowledge, then alone will it be an accomplishment at the mental level. All too soon, one may feel the urge to go away from the environment in which one is living, but unless the right knowledge has been imbibed by then, suppression of urges will be the result and not sublimation of desire. Such suppressions will fume and froth unseen, as the lava in the bowels of the brooding volcano, and the hour will come when the chained fury will break its bonds and erupt. Destruction can be the only result. Far better that the seeker should come to believe deeply the mastery of mind over matter, and cultivate dissociation from the environment while living and working in it as before.

You have been caught, oh mind, caught by the hand of this sacred land. The valley is the palm, and the hills the fingers that have fastened their clasp at your throat. But you are not easily vanquished, many are the tricks you know. Taking recourse to the wings of memory, you seek to escape. Do your worst, mind, for I shall not let you succeed. The time for reckoning has come.

So where will you go? To the City? All right, rip the veil of fantasy and falsehood and see it for what it is – this city, where Materialism must stage its last fight against the seeker who stands poised to scale the lonely, yet lovely, peaks of new knowledge, where objectivity holds her vanity fair to display all her glittering wares of polished tinsel and paste diamonds! What of real worth has she to offer me? I see the vulgarity of her vain riches. I hear the pathetic emptiness of her loud laughter; her greatest delights are bubbles that burst at the touch. just as a harlot, frantic at the impending departure of the long- deceived lover now grown wise, might in desperation flaunt her faded nakedness before him, hoping to tempt him back into her false embrace, too foolish to know that his awakened mind is further repulsed by the very attitude that seeks to attract him. So too is it here attempted, and in vain. Therefore, mind, you shall return to the valley with me. Listen to me, mind, listen, or you have no salvation. All your goodness will not gain you freedom, for ethics alone cannot free you from the bondage of Time. Time will ensnare you and make you a slave for eternity. So heed my words. You must learn to stop Time. To do so, search for the Present. What is Real must exist in the Present, what exists in the past must be unreal. And the future? Oh, it is but the Present bulging out in its desires and expectations!! Mind, mind, look at yourself. Are you only Memory, mind? If so, you are a dead phantom, a ghost, a myth, a delusion. Shall I yield my right to you, I to whom the Present belongs? No, no, no....

Mother, is it you? I thought there was an instant now when Time stood still and you were beside me, and the Silence yielded its secret song to the silence in my soul. It seemed the worlds paused in their gyrations, halted by a will they could not disobey. The river flows again, Mother, and the winds have resumed their mighty sweep, terrific is the motion of mute planets through immeasurable space as they rush along their charted courses. Oh mighty spectacle, bewildering, bewitching, beautiful! Let the storm rage, for now I am at the centre where there is only Shanti, Shanti, Shanti.

48
Thoughts on Gandhi and Nehru

Nehru was the Prime-Minister of India since 1947. He died on May 27, 1964 and this article was written then.

For himself, he died in the morning; but for us, he died in the afternoon, the breath having lingered awhile through his state of coma. He had accepted, but the nation needed time to prepare itself for the inevitable. So he tarried. Was it not ever thus? He would have been one thing for himself, he had to be somewhat another for the people. Perception set him upon the peaks, performance held him upon the plateau.

But man is not two things, nor many things, but the one thing that is the sum-total of his entire mental life. There are no truths apart from my concepts, there are no duties to others that are not duties to myself, and I never serve others but only serve my timeless will. Time compels my mind and my mind compels me. That is the truth of man. And so we saw him with his feet upon the air, and we regretted that he was not on firm land. But his regret was – and ours should have been – that he had not hauled himself to the summit which his out-stretched hands could touch. Sense of duty and doership were rocks tied to his feet. Love for the people lay heavily upon him.

Not so with Gandhiji. Love for the people lay lightly upon him, for it was but a reflection of his love for God. His abode was upon the peak, and his pleasure upon the plains. He wandered effortlessly and acted without willing. The means of Truth he pursued, and witnessed the ends as they came. That love can bring sorrow, that truth can invite seeming disaster, was known to him long ago, for he had understood how all this too is Love and Love is Truth.

So, in our ignorance, we at times accused Gandhiji of limited vision, for our own limits did not encompass the full panorama of relativity as his did. Yet we could not escape the compelling power of his purity, and we gave him our hearts. None more so than his heir, Nehru.

Panditji gave his heart to the Mahatma and took it back with his benediction, but he could not bring himself to surrender his head. Alas, there are aspects of Love and Truth that the keenest intellect cannot comprehend. To know that the ultimate accomplishment of the intellect is not to think but to silence itself one must hearken with deep reverence to the Rishis of our ancient land.

What is true of Panditji is more grossly true of our nation. We have a heart that unknowingly turns to God, but a mind that is one-half misapprehension and one half non-apprehension. We postulate political theories that dimly echo the wisdom of the Vedas from our unconscious heritage, but at the conscious level of implementation, we waver, compromise and descend. We assume the courage of gods when we pledge ourselves to non-alignment, but yield to the fear of mortals when our physical existence is threatened. Doubts arise whether one can remain detached as witness (*Sakshi matra*), and the age-old myth of happiness in attachment woos us with siren song. Where a Gandhiji may remain blissfully unarmed, a

Panditji cannot but rise in dynamic defiance. Both would sooner lead the nation to death than to dishonour and thus to life and honour beyond death – but how different would be their inner springs of strength.

We lift up our hand, with Panch-Sheela[4] in our hearts, palm and fingers held as if to bless. But when the other signatory replies with the hand held somewhat alike but threateningly as if to push us back, we lose conviction in our virtue and land in the mid-air of doubts.

Our tragedy is not that we are not good – our moral heritage should distinguish us as the greatest nation in the world today – but that we lack the conviction of our goodness. And lacking conviction, we lack courage. This is because godliness lingers in our blood and bones as an inescapable aspect of this "Punya-bhoomi" (sanctified land) but is not adequately available to us at the conscious level to instruct our attitudes and actions.

On the one hand there are nations whose political morality has not yet attained even to the level of common ethics, and the world sees them floundering in the netherlands of nowhere. On the other, here is a nation that has risen above the level of such average conduct, but having failed to grasp securely the pinnacles we aspired to, is also seen to be neither here nor there. If the world equates the two, it need not disturb us, but the thought that frightens is: Are we ourselves doing so? The arc may deride the circle as being beginningless, endless, and therefore meaningless, but how shall the knower of the circle doubt where perfection lies?

Thus we see that Panditji was the most perfect personification of our imperfect state, that he belonged beautifully to the times, that he contained in himself India's destiny of today and direction of

4 A doctrinaire declaration shared by India and China to ensure peace and trust. But a war followed.

tomorrow. With one foot amidst us, and one foot ahead of us, symbolising security and motion, and eyes looking beyond our gaze, he led and we followed.

We loved him without the confusion of reverence. How we loved him! Witness this last homage of multitudes, the tearful thousands that throng for one glimpse of the urn that contains a portion of the ashes. How then must he have loved us that this should be so? Could a lesser love have begotten this reciprocal love of millions? No. The cause is ever greater than the effect.

The mind, approaching perfection, arrives at a point where the unity in creation becomes a living force. A limitless love is thereby engendered. This is the first quarter of salvation as vouchsafed by meditation upon Pranava (the sacred AUM).

"The first quarter (Pada) is Vaiswanara whose sphere of activity is the waking state, who is conscious of the external world of objects... One who knows this attains the fulfillment of all his desires and becomes the first or the foremost among all... "

– Mandukya Upanishad: stanzas 3 & 9

Such a one was Panditji. Never mind what he said about religion. Truth is not altered by opinion. Religion functions in society only to create men like him. His words may decry religion but his life vindicates it. That again is the contradiction that he had ever to be.

Gandhiji knew this and more. Surely he was living in the higher order of the second quarter.

"The second quarter (Pada) is Taijasa whose sphere of activity is the Dream-state, who is conscious of the internal world of objects He who knows this attains to a superior knowledge".

– *Mandukya Upanishad: stanzas 4 & 10*

The unity within creation is the unity within a dream. The joy and sorrow and redemption of life is the joy, sorrow and redemption of a dream. Knowing this was the step that separated the two, the King and the Prince.

Panditji saw that discontent must remain and become a positive urge leading to progress. Gandhiji knew that, even more truly, horizons are never reached but are for ever receding; that peace, plenty, and perfection must be found here and not yonder, and that indeed it can be so. Hence, the one dreamt of giant machines in turbulent motion, the other smiled behind the spinning wheel.

Ramakrishna Paramahamsa cast his mantle on Vivekananda, but chained him with duty to stumbling mankind. The Master, who was Perfection, desired that his heir should fulfil himself through service and activity – and then society, lifted and blessed for a while, would be left to work out its destiny with lesser or larger lights.

Gandhiji groomed his heir and perhaps hoped in his heart that through a life of sacrifice and service his favourite disciple would discover the higher laws of Providence which demand as the price of revelation the ultimate sacrifice of one's ego and the surrender of one's sense of doership. But this did not come to pass.

Panditji, for whom the failings of the nation were a personal burden, fretted and fumed at the superstition of the ignorant, and when he spoke in condemnation of religion he spoke of dead routines of ritualistic activity; when of faith, of irrational wishfulness; when of prayer, of irreverential selfishness. In his righteous human anger, he did not stop to concede that here were great words basely used and great purposes grossly applied. The noble faith of our forefathers, the fervent prayers of our rishis, the mighty rituals of our vedas – these are divinised perfections of mind and method, these still abide in our country, these give us our nation-hood, our culture and our tradition as they course often unsuspected through our veins. It is of these that Panditji unknowingly spoke in spite of himself when in vague terms he referred to a mysterious Force beyond naming. It is these that unseen beckoned him when he pondered over the Gita or read the words of Sri Sankara. So he knew and did not know.

And now he is gone. That is half the statement. He is gone and I remain – that alone is the complete statement. It is time to think of myself.

The renowned and redoubtable elder statesman, Sri C. Rajagopalachari wrote: "Eleven years younger than me, eleven times more important for the nation, and eleven hundred times more beloved of the nation, Sri Nehru has suddenly departed; the old guard-room is completely empty now..."

When Gandhiji died, I thought of human sin and wept. When Kennedy died, I thought of Kennedy and wept. Now Panditji is dead, and I think of myself and weep. And here I come closest to progress. If love is spent in vain and volatile tears, what remains? It is time for action, action which will give expression to a love for the living as the most beautiful tribute to the love for the departed.

Oh God, give me sincerity. Save me from the banality of words, and from complacency. Twice you have sent light to lead me, once through Gandhiji who knew that God was man, and then through Panditji who believed that Man was God. Now let me march...

49
Totally Predictable Acrimony Over Astrology

(In The Year 2000)

The gusty gutsy winds of verbal violence emanating from a disturbance in the Chief of UGC seem to have abated for the present, though the monsoon may not be over. The move by the University Grants Commission to introduce academic courses in astrology in universities led (predictably) to outbursts of heat and light from a galaxy of stars upon our earth, scientists and intellectuals and rationalists. THE HINDU covered the turbulence fairly objectively, giving space and opportunity to both sides in a debate that needlessly narrowed down to Raman Vs Raman (Dr. C.V. Raman, the great scientist and Dr. B.V. Raman, the great astrologist).

Granted the need arose for comment on the perceived priorities at the decision-making level on re-structuring and reforming higher education in our country. Anger and emphasis should have focused on exigencies, limitations, and results. India, long neglected, needs a hundred remedies and revivals of which a few are crying desperately for attention, and the rest have to yield and wait. "A" for Astronomy need not head the list of priorities.

But to denigrate, defile, and deny a wealth of unique and ancient wisdom, hastily applying half-defined parameters of chosen disciplines to condemn it, is not in keeping with intellectual dignity. This knife cuts with both edges. Let national activity proceed diligently for maximum utility.

In the progressive quest for knowledge about the universe, science deals with matter, and with energies that act on matter. Mind, whatever the word connotes, cannot be ignored. Mind, which is everyone's personal asset and experience, is naturally sensed as the intimation of consciousness. This consciousness is the essence of a living person, the power to know, remember, respond to stimuli – in short be self-aware and by that token, aware of all else. Without the existence of consciousness, where would abide the existence of matter? In itself? Does it not mean matter knows itself? Is that acceptable as a statement?

But science insists that brain PRODUCES consciousness, that what is collectively called mind is a product of neural and chemical activity. It declares that our subjectively felt and confirmed sentiency is produced by the insentient inert atoms and molecules of which the physical brain is made, because of the configuration of those molecules.

When this is questioned, the other stream of inquiry is denoted by words like spiritual, astral, or mystical. It is objected that such an inquiry may yield conjecture, imagination or faith as distinct from fact, but no provable data-base.

With no pretense to originality I am trying to re-group ideas and reframe the conclusions that already exist, but may be dispersed and diffused.

Creation is, at source, one fact, one event, one reality. If matter was primordial soup, there was no choice on the menu card! If change was there (and still is) time and chance are not the operative words, the word is "energy". This energy has names in science, such as gravity, electromagnetism, heat or radiation. But select one word and one concept of energy, as we must, and that would be gravitational-field. If that is not precise, science can call it the UNIFIED-FIELD.

But what about the energy of consciousness, which co-exists with creation, and must be merged in the holistic reckoning? Science has not come to terms with this statement. It cannot, because it has not considered mentation as an energy-system.

If apples can confirm to us the energy of gravity, should not "thoughts" that are dropping all the time and in all space ("time" and "space" themselves being our thoughts) reveal to us the energy of consciousness? So it is said that the cosmos is a CONSCIOUSNESS-FIELD. Science which sees space pervaded and possessed by gravity, can consider this field to be "self-aware space". With some liberty I will borrow the language of the energy-field of matter-science, and say in the energy-field of mental-science thoughts are the particles, concepts are the molecules, and deeds are the agglomerates. AS WE THINK, SO WE ACT. AS WE ACT, SO IS THE DESTINY OF HUMANITY SHAPED. Thought-particles are being moved in consciousness-field.

Any body is made up of what was consumed as food. From sperm to embryo to infant to the fat fellow, all the cells were the rearrangement of food consumed. Anything emerging from the body as sweat, urine, faeces, saliva, is from the same origin. So thoughts, described as the finest subtlest essence of food, are of the category of particles. [Quality of food a person eats influences the quality of his mind.]

We are talking of the energy of consciousness. In ultimate terms of time, space, and causal determinism, all energies must obey one law; otherwise there would be randomness, conflict and chaos. Gravity acting on masses of matter with infallible constancy determines the disposition of planets and galaxies. The sun is where it is, and our earth is where it is, and the two relate the way they do, because gravity is exactly and always, what it is. Any variation, and it would be a different story, or no story! Our planet would be frozen to death or charred to death, So gravity is what seals the fate of the material earth. Call it the karma of this planet (or any other planet) if you wish.

What is "gravity" in the world of matter is "karma" in the mental world. As gravity causes and controls events from Black Holes to expanding universes, gravity in the mental frame becomes the karmic energy, shaping thinking and acting and behaving, and thus determining the events of human history. It is this energy system that Astrology deals with and calculates.

Bodies of matter are subject to gravitational attraction, the effect being determined in terms of the mass of the bodies, and the distance between them. The fact that ocean tides are measurably disturbed during full-moon and new-moon, when the relative alignment of earth and moon maximizes the impact of the gravitational forces, fully establishes the effect of gravity on matter. Scientists know that the mental behaviour of some humans (already delicately balanced) suffers tidal disturbances on the same occasions. What is the common factor? It is the factor of gravity.

I am not a student of astrology and am living securely without it. But so do I live in respect of E=mc2. I do not need that either for my secure living. From my general understanding, astrology seems to work out the resolution of gravitational forces, (using its exclusive if archaic nomenclature,) on the mind of the subject-person. The equation will depend on the masses, distances, and angles of the massive bodies in space, and also the "mass" and "density" of the thought – particles (the units of the mind). The location of planets in their orbits and their configuration with respect to our earth keep changing. Each configuration will deliver a different vector of forces as the resultant. The mind is conditioned to that extent. In turn, actions are conditioned. And since actions make the man, it is said that his destiny is conditioned. But this is not the whole story. This deals with one aspect. It is the external influence. Loosely it is called "fate". A better classification is "Prarabda Karma". It is not ultimate. There is energy in the personal consciousness of the individual. It has the power of "free-will". It can counter, control and command. This is called "Purushartha". Nowhere is it the council of despair. If individualized personality is conceded, then free-will must be admitted.

To retort that huge celestial bodies cannot be concerned about a puny mortal on earth, is a petty and undignified argument. As one diamond can possess a value that a mountain of rock cannot, one fleeting thought-impulse of sentiency in the mind of man is a greater wonder in creation that the temporal eternity of massive insentient stars.

Beyond this point the discussion will mutate into "spirituality". Matter and mind have been seen as coeval aspects of creation, and the highest reach of inquiry into creation may reveal the truth of relativity, but not the truth of Absolutism. (Einstein has agreed by naming his conclusions of cosmic reality, the theory of "relativity", not of "absolutism".) Spirituality reaches for the Absolute which is no longer a mode of information but of experience. The sages, it is believed, LIVE and state that truth. Let us recall the words of one such, who could provoke, and intuit us into deeper understanding. (quoted from "I AM THAT" of Nisargadatta Maharaj.)

The sage is explaining that Total Consciousness (of which time, space, and causation are but the contents) is the origin and abode of all creation; that its presence and fullness is in the self-awareness of I; there is no one without I-AM-ness as the basis; and the rediscovery must focus there. The sage says: "You are talking of the temporary, while I am dealing with the eternal. Gods and their universes come and go, avatars follow each other, and in the end we are back at the source. I talk only of the timeless source of all the gods with all their universes, past, present, and future".

The student retaliates: "Do you know them all? Do you remember them?"

Sage: "When a few boys stage a play for fun, what is there to see and remember?"

The calculated irreverence of the statement guides the seeker deeper into self-inquiry, as does Ramana Maharshi's famed pointer, "WHO AM I?" That is the soul of Vedanta, but it is not today our cup of tea. We will go now to what the sage said within the reach of relativity. He is explaining causation, the cause-effect operation. He is talking of the power and potential of the mind, the principle of consciousness, the gravity that science will endorse when it has put together the now elusive Theory of Everything (TOE). The sage says: "There is only a holistic wholeness. Everything is the cause and everything is the effect. THE STARS INFLUENCE YOU, BUT YOU INFLUENCE THE STARS TOO."

[We saw the moon tug at the ocean-drop. Was not the ocean-drop tugging at the moon too?]

Therefore we are not merely the hunted, we are hunters too. The astrologers amongst angels in heaven must right now be busy recasting the HOROSCOPE OF SATURN. They must be drawing diagrams. "There are powerful omens on earth. A dangerous one has shifted house in Central Asia. A benevolent one is neutralized by opposing forces in the rasi called Parliament. A corrupt one may snatch the golden reins of power elsewhere. Cricket has been stumped. Oil has become terror-ible. Saturn has a bad destiny for a decade of years. He must beware the human".

Shall we leave the worrying to the planets (serves them right at last) and get on with the serious business of nation-building?

50
A Sanyasi

A mind that revolts against what it perceives may bring about a revolution, which must only flatter to deceive. A mind that revolts against its own lack of perception, brings about evolution, which endures and elevates.

Restless waves, pounding in futile fury against the unyielding shore. And the "back-waters", a labyrinth of water-ways, calm and serene beneath the swaying palms, part of the tumultuous ocean and yet a scheme apart. That is Kerala, the west coast of the Southern peninsula of India. Was this land itself moulded as a comprehensive symbol of the contradictory mind of man; as the sea, heaving and panting in eternal despair, forever unable to overrun the limiting shores of destiny, and yet forever unable to desist from the helpless movement; and, as the back-waters, still and silent in its extensions, no different in content but so different in construction?

There, some years ago, in what was then a princely state, was born in a respected and affluent family, the child of this narrative, that grew up as a favourite of the *kulagurus* (family preceptors). To the wakeful, early dawn heralds the tarrying sun. To the holy teachers, was the glorious future already discernible?

Kerala is the land of fragrant tradition and flowery ritual, the land that has cradled many a spiritual giant from the era of Adi Sankara. This boy, scarce six or seven years old, had to submit to a daily drill at dusk of nearly two hours, while pooja (worship) was performed. The diffused wrath of a distant God could perchance be dared, but not the sudden sting of a cruel cane within ready reach of the *cheriyammas* (aunts) who presided over the function. Therefore, he spent the crawling moments listlessly gazing at the many pictures of deities, in awe, in ridicule, in amusement, or in confusion – till the picture of Siva held his gaze, to the exclusion of all else, so peaceful was His countenance, so tender His smile, so loving and lovable every aspect of Him. And the boy learnt to close his eyes, thus to see more clearly, more vividly, more intimately, in the sightless recesses of his own inner being, the kindly Presence whose redeeming grace would transform him twenty years later.

Adolescence brought freedom from aunts and anachronisms. Time was spent at school or on the beaches, in play or in friendships, but daily worship faded away. Only, between wakefulness and sleep there was a brief but beautiful moment of communion with Him and His love.

Youth brought a quickening of the intellect – was it an awakening, or an arrogance? – and the subdued surrender of boyhood to unexplained symbolism now gave way to the cynical superiority of a vengeful mind. Am I an extension of God, or is God a creature of my creation? He argued, and conveniently content with apparent rationality, suited his own answer to his needs and plunged into life to seek pleasure, success, fame and fortune. To the brilliant handsome witty and virile young man, trailing academic degrees after his name, the things he sought came easily, and for a while society opened its treasure-chest for him. But as he fondled the gems he had so longed for, he saw there the degraded glitter of tinsel, the wayward wealth of spurious imitation, the optical deception of coloured beads. Shall I mortgage all my life for more of these? he asked.

The gaze turned inwards. And he felt deeply: Beloved Lord, whoever you are, whatever you are, wherever you are, in some sense you are me too, an integral part that cannot be lost. This touch of your Being is more enduring and more rewarding than everything that life outside can offer me.

Once it had seemed enough to laugh and play upon this earth, but that was in the innocence of childish fulfillments. In the adult world of pleasures and passions, of pursuit and possession, love was but lust, charity but conceit, truth a convenience, virtue a compromise. A false eternity was filled with time, and frightened humanity moved towards a troubled death desperately seeking water in a mirage. The youth stood apart and saw all this. And the movement within commenced. The burdensome imposition of boyhood prayers now returned as a welcome practice to soothe the wounds of the bruised adult. The Japa (saying the beads) came back to him, not in a spirit of defeatism, but with the refreshing realisation that he was stepping out on to the path of Life Divine.

He took to an intense study of philosophy, both Indian and Western. But brief spells of intellectual satisfaction only revealed wider areas of discontent and discord. A faith that would not be denied, and a devotion that could not be verbalized, strained at the leash for self-expression. He left the dry polymics of a laboured philosophy, and taught himself to be good and do good; to serve, love, purify, meditate, realise, and be free. Practice of these became life to him, and existence in the same abhorred Palace of life acquired a new meaning and stood out as a new opportunity.

Some years passed thus again. And again the discontent grew. An ancient ache was rising, a forgotten melody was returning, a dormant destiny came awake and calling. He began to think of life in an Ashram, a deliberate and total identification with Lord Siva who was biding His time within the heart. He bent his hesitant steps towards the mountains and was accepted in an Ashram.

The new life seemed to have all the peace and beauty that his tormented heart had sought. But could this too be a deception? On the rebound from an indulgent, insensitive, and greedy society, was he deluding himself into ascribing positive, dynamic, enduring values to the stillness of a graveyard, the meekness of a coward, or the charity of a bankrupt? He watched himself for several days, and slowly the conviction grew that this is it, this is what my soul has longed for, the path to my fulfulment; beyond all doubt, this is it. And so he took sanyas (the order of renunciation). The Swami was born.

In the Himalayan ranges, over 100 miles form the cities of the plains at an altitude of about 5000 feet, where flows the river Bhageerathi which in lower regions becomes the Holy Ganga, in a tiny dwelling upon a hilly slope, resided a spiritual colossus whose glory a continent could hardly contain, adored by all the saints and sages of the land, revelling in the serene silence and scenic splendour of the mountains, his fame soaring higher than the snow-clad peaks around him. To this renowned Teacher of teachers went the Sanyasi, already initiated but yet thirsting for knowledge, seeking, striving, daring.

Oh, the pain, the intensity, the sweet ecstasy of this yearning for liberation from the vanities and thraldom of life, so that you collect all your energies in one great longing and take the plunge! There was a vacant kingdom, in search of a king.

Nine summers he spent at the feet of his Master, being taught, loved, rebuked and adored, always and again led forward firmly towards the Truth of one's own self, which being discerned, the harmony of infinite space and eternal time stands revealed.

Years passed and he was secure in the armour of his knowledge. There was in him the abiding peace of mind freed from the compulsion of motley desires; yet, the memory of those he had left behind upon the plains of mundane living came back to him, causing sorrow born of sheer love of humanity. They had been just like him, intelligent and energetic, eager to succeed and having no measure of success except in terms of pomp, power, and possessions, fighting their unequal battles against time. The best of them sinned without knowing, and suffered without understanding. He had saved himself or had been saved, and the subtle secret had been revealed to him that "without body you cannot be killed, without possessions you cannot be robbed, without mind you cannot be deceived". The grace of his Master had unravelled for him the true content of the Upanishads, the Bhagawad Gita, and the Bhasyas, and he stood supreme as the point of Awareness that witnessed the body, the possessions, the mind. But he had to return by his own persuasion to the arena he had abandoned, and involve himself again in the destinies of those who, left to themselves, would make of their lives no more than brief gasps of pain between birth and death. The pundits, discoursing upon the scriptures, were caught in the superficialities of words and vain argument. The need was to expound the intrinsic nature of all experience, and show the intimate truth of personal existence here and now. He knew it, and knew that he knew it, yet could he convey the subtle truth to crowds in the market-places of civilisation? He stood in doubt upon the banks of the river. And suddenly it came upon him that Mother Ganga, born of the mountains, was decisively rushing to the plains, a source of life and nourishment, seeking fulfillment in giving. He felt reassured.

The master gave a hesitant approval to the pleadings of his brilliant disciple: not that he doubted the will or wisdom of his ward, but because he knew how mighty and diabolical could be the cumulative power of prejudice and perjury, of sloth and superstition, of habit and ritual. Had not Christ been nailed upon a cross? Yet he graciously blessed the youngster and freed him on his chosen path.

The Sanyasi packed up his dream and stepped out. He would talk in the idiom of the educated masses, he would invite their critical assessment as he led them from the known into the knowable. And if orthodoxy was desperately scheming its own perpetuation though deprived of meaning or devoid of nobler purpose, why, he would save the people from orthodoxy and save orthodoxy from itself. He would revive the vibrant culture of his ancient land.

That was then.

At the early gatherings, a handful sat around the Sadhu[5], curious, cynical, or hopeful. The bug bit them all! Word spread of the clarity of thought, the cascade of words, the cadence of laughter. And above all, the intimate relevance of the theme to personal living, elevating, strengthening, and integrating the individual. So they came in larger and larger numbers, and were grateful to him that gave, were happy in their own ability to receive. Inspired by success and exhilarated by the loving response, he poured all his energies into the giving and raced across the land like a whirlwind, sweeping aside the slumber of generations.

The mind has no limitations, but the body has its. This incessant toil of compassion must demand its price from the flesh. The rarest phenomenon only reveals and confirms the subtler validity of the same ageless laws and the exception proves the rule. So it happened in due course, and that it had not happened earlier was the wonder. In a climax of physical anguish, the heart faltered, life flickered, time froze in its stride – God, dear God, please, dear God – then again spring stayed with him, and time resumed its march. He had survived the massive cardiac attack.

---

5 Holy man.

The impersonal sun sheds its light; seeing is our effort. But the guru is bound by his personal mission of mercy to open our eyes, to clear our sight, and to give us the light that illumines. He succeeds because he is so intensely involved. He cannot be rejected by us, because he does not set himself apart from us. Ever joyous, he knows the problem of our sorrow. Ever peaceful, he understands the conflicts of our personality. He does not beckon to us from distant peaks, but holds our hand upon the rugged path in the foothills of our upward journey, and guides us one sure step at a time.

The Perfect One, whoever he is, is not known by outward signs. What is seen, heard, and known is only an idea determined by the conditioned mind of the knower. It is futile to look for true ideas – there aren't any! He can be of any form, respond in any manner, decide in any way. It proves nothing about him, but inviolably presents to us the universal harmony of that instant. He is ever natural, and sees naturalness alone everywhere, but to those that have misunderstood themselves to be cripples, he will reveal the potent power of their own limbs. He tempts us with crutches only to make us walk on our legs.

To hundreds of thousands he shows the possibility and the path. He invites the questioning mind to protest against compulsive tradition, to scoff at empty ritual, to challenge time-worn dogma. Every concept is analysed and revalued in terms of personal experience of the listener. No second step is forced unless the first is conceded by teacher and taught to be rational. Heaven and hell shall wait till we are clear about reactions and results. Destiny shall remain patient while the working of cause-and-effect relationship is intimately understood. Evolution shall stay suspended till the interplay of mind and matter has been unravelled. And when the anatomy of one thought, one experience, has been thoroughly laid bare, shall I not find therein the answer to the ultimate riddle of the Creator and the created?

Were he a mere scholar of unusual learning, he would at best engender intellectual satisfactions that linger awhile. But love generates love, fosters a sense of identity in which becoming gains precedence over knowing. That is why so many feel an enraptured impulse to follow in his footprints.

I hear the merry laughter that I have never forgotten. Were he by me now, he would say:

Like a bird on its wings, I leave no footprints.

That is the paradox of the Guru.

51
The Hype and The Happening

Once this did happen. A running race was organized at a festival of life in the forests, between a hare and a tortoise. It was truly recorded that the tortoise won. Some animals at the starting line had seen the tortoise's lumbering start, as the hare sprinted ahead round a curve. At the other end of the winding course another group of animals, standing there, had seen the tortoise cross the line while the hare came desperately running behind. No one had seen the whole event from start to finish, which would have given the true perspective. No animal had a watch to know how much time had elapsed during the race. They just concluded that the tortoise had accelerated in overdrive for most of the stretch, and won.

As the legend spread, the sports committee presented a victory medal to the tortoise, which he never took off his chest.

Growing progressively arrogant, he decided to challenge the hare again next year.

During the first race last year, a crow had flown over the whole course back and forth and seen the complacent hare settle down for a leisurely nap part way up the race, yawning and muttering "This is child's play. I have all the time in the forest world." And had over-slept. The crow was the only one who knew the real event and he crowed his advise to the tortoise, but the tortoise rejected it. "I did it once. I can do it again" was the retort. And he fondled his medal.

The race was run. When the hare crossed the distant finishing line, the tortoise had covered nine yards, three inches. Spectators sulked away in silence without looking at each other. The crow laughed and laughed.

But this is not just a laughing matter. It is a zen story of deep philosophic import to warn human animals in their samsaric jungles against tamasic indulgence or egotistical doership.

52
Epilogue.
To Mother Saraswathi

Shall I stand still, wondering what benevolence lights my path – and waste the blessed moment? No, Mother. That you love me is enough. Mother, Thy grace has revealed to me glimpses of Thy mysterious creation, sufficient to know that no greater happiness or fulfillment can this life yield to me than that I spend it in surrender to Thee.

Mother, You led me through all the cravings that throng the human breast and allowed me to indulge in them. Yet through the years that could have blinded and bound me for ever, You spared me with a saving grace of which I knew nothing then. You placed me amongst the exalted, but when their quick departure might have left me in lonely despair, You gave me the reassuring light of a new knowledge.

And suddenly one day I knew, Mother, that I would never lose You, and that nothing else mattered.

I have heard Your speech in the silence of my heart, and felt the caressing touch of Your tender fingers in tears trickling down the cheeks.

I know too well, Mother, how unworthy I have been of such grace. You have revealed many things to my mind and been patient with me, yet I permit the years to go by without determination, without courage, without adequate purpose – which means, without gratitude, does it not?

How can I ask for forgiveness, remaining unchanged? And if changed, then what need for forgiveness?

Mother, You charged me with the duty of fulfilling my allotted work of writing these articles, to make it an instrument wherewith to teach me. To whom shall I tell how profitable the pursuit has been for my evolution! Now the task ceases. Mother, upon the path that my faltering feet will henceforth pace, shed Thy kindly light. In the darkness of ignorance that so densely shrouds me yet, cast a ray or two to save me still.

And may the Perfect Son of Divinity, Lord Ganesha[6] who lent me faculties not my own, find me still worthy of His blessings, and guide my steps.

– Om –

6 Ganesha is the deity whose grace is insvoked for removal of obstacles.

Other Books by Dwaraknath Reddy

1. The Dicey Problem of New Age Science
   (Einstein, Hawking and God at the Casino)

   "God does not play dice" said Einstein. "God is quite a gambler" was Stephen Hawking's note of dissent. These famous quotes discuss whether Newtonian determinism or quantum probability is the truth in creation. But Truth or Reality cannot be extracted from relativity. It is Absolute. Therefore it needs to be said "God has no need to play dice, for HE OWNS THE CASINO. His right hand picks up what the left hand may lose. Our situation is different." The author establishes this significance; through extension, not contradiction.

2. Death Was Never Born Life Never Died
   (Reincarnation or Evolution?)

   Total Consciousness, absolute, undivided, eternal, is the source, the Reality. (Another word for it is God). In creation it is within the experience of each one of us as MIND. It is an illusory distorted presentation of Pure Consciousness, now seen as a dim reflection in a flawed mirror. That is the *person* – you and me. Cosmic existence and experience is the voyage of desire, action, and reaction, till the error of limitation is overcome. The finale is the return to perfection. (Enlightenment, Realization, are other words for it.) The investigation examines evolution, "life-after-death," reincarnation, memory, sub-conscience, et al, and peeps over the horizon at Transcendence.

3. **Can God Improve my Balance-Sheet?**
(Invoking the inner potential)

A book of Business Management Psychology, social and self management included (rather, self first).

4. **Gentle breeze, rustling leaves**
(Sing, my soul, your symphony of silence)

Gentle breezes blow across the mind, caressing the leaves of contemplation, emotion and wonder. The ego and the companion-self are in intimate conversation. Slowly the winds rest in space, the rustling sounds sink into silence.

5. **The Physics of Karma** *(A Requiem to Time)*

Karma is the causal rightness in all events and sequences in creation. Karma is the operating law of the energy of Total Consciousness. It is one stream, one movement, engulfing all of cosmic creation. It is the cause and methodology of all forces playing on the material universe and the mental universe. It includes all the physical laws defined by time, space and causation, and establishes the identical laws at work on the mental plane. It then reveals its transcendental supremacy as the source, the Absolute. The workings of Karma can be unravelled by every one of us in terms of our daily life.

6. **Diving Deep into Ramana Maharshi's Teachings**

7. **Divya, The Rainbow Child** *(Fiction)*

8. **Sumangali** *(Fiction)*

www.ingramcontent.com/pod-product-compliance
Ingram Content Group UK Ltd.
Pitfield, Milton Keynes, MK11 3LW, UK
UKHW021906190726
13853UKWH00002B/541